CONTENTS

Bhutan's Buddhist Architecture

Written and published by Laura Blake

Text, photographs, maps, and drawings created by the author; except for map bases, provided by and copyrighted by Map Resources; photograph of Cave 26, Ajanta by Dey.sandip (Own work) [CC BY-SA 3.0 (http://creativecommons.org/licenses/by-sa/3.0)], via Wikimedia Commons; photograph of Lalitagiri by Daniel Limma (Own work) [CC BY-SA 3.0 (http://creativecommons.org/licenses/by-sa/3.0)], via Wikimedia Commons; and photographs of Jokhang Temple and Sayme Monastery, provided by Cathy Ann Taylor, Catarra LLC. Front and back cover images show details of Punakha Dzong.

Laura@LauraBlakeArchitect.com

Edited by Robin Jacobson
Consultation by Jeff Durham, Assistant Curator of Himalayan Art, Asian Art Museum

First edition 2015
Printed by CreateSpace, an Amazon.com Company
ISBN 978-0-9966639-0-8

Laura Blake earned a Bachelor of Arts in Art History from Brown University and a Master of Architecture from the University of California, Los Angeles. A practicing architect with a specialty in buildings for public use, Laura has a keen interest in world cultures, their architectural traditions, and their great and enduring religious and civic buildings.

Kirtimukha, Punakha Dzong

Introduction

When I first visited Bhutan, I found myself lingering at each Buddhist temple, monastery, and dzong, savoring the beauty of the simple stone structures and their elaborate woodwork, and wondering about the origin of the architectural style and the meaning of the symbols decorating the woodwork. Curious, I looked for but could not find a source that provided the information I sought, so I decided to write *Bhutan's Buddhist Architecture*. I hope this book, which may be read as an introduction or used as a guide while traveling, helps readers better understand Bhutan's sacred buildings, their rich symbolism, and their magical history.

The book begins with brief historical and architectural overviews. The former describes how Buddhism emerged, spread across Asia, and reached Bhutan—and how Bhutan then evolved into a Buddhist state. The latter describes Indian and Tibetan precedents that influenced Bhutan's Buddhist architecture, and characteristics typical of its temples, monasteries and dzongs—the fortresses built while Bhutan was being unified as a Buddhist state. The next sections provide examples of these buildings. Each example includes a description of the building's founding, configuration, and one or two of its notable features, and is illustrated with a plan and photographs. The last section introduces symbols commonly used in building decoration. Each symbol has a brief description and a photograph.

Those visiting Bhutan will likely notice differences between what is shown in this book and what they see at that time. This is because, as has been done for centuries, buildings are regularly renovated to repair damage, accommodate new needs, or for patronage. Also readers may notice differences in dates, data, spellings, and descriptions of legends and symbols. This is because sources vary. In Bhutan, where legends are part of history, and impermanence is integral to life, meaning can be more important than information. I have tried to use the most authoritative sources for dates, data and spelling as well as the most common descriptions of legends and symbols, and to prepare clear maps and plans. Any mistakes are my own.

I would like to thank Mountain Travel Sobek, and their Bhutanese partner Snow Leopard Trekking Company, for introducing me to Bhutan; Geographic Expeditions and their Bhutanese partner Yangphel Adventure Travel for an inspiring tour across Bhutan; and Yeoong Tours and Travels for two remarkable trips visiting temples, monasteries and dzongs. I am grateful to John Stucky, Librarian of the Asian Art Museum; Jeff Durham, Assistant Curator of Himalayan Art of the Asian Art Museum; and Robin Jacobson, editor for their assistance as I worked on this book. Finally, I would like to thank my parents Liz and Igor Blake, who introduced me to the joy of traveling and learning about different cultures and their art and architecture.

Laura Blake
San Francisco, 2015

HISTORICAL OVERVIEW

The Zhabdrung, Gangte Goemba

Bhutan is a small Himalayan country with a rich and enduring Buddhist heritage. The following historical overview describes how Buddhism emerged, spread across Asia, and reached Bhutan; how Bhutan developed and unified as a Buddhist state, and how Buddhism is practiced in Bhutan today.

Buddhism emerges and spreads[1]

In the fifth century BCE Siddhartha Gautama, a prince in northern India, became a wandering ascetic in search of the true nature of existence. Like many of his contemporaries, he believed that life and death were a continuum in which one's actions determined one's next rebirth. However he did not find true understanding in the elaborate rituals of Brahmanism, an early form of Hinduism popular in the region at the time, or in the extreme physical hardship of his fellow ascetics. After much reflection, he realized that ignorance caused suffering and that one could overcome ignorance and attain enlightenment by meditating and leading a virtuous life. He became known as the Buddha (one who is awake), and spent the rest of his life teaching others what he had learned.

Buddhism gradually became popular, spreading throughout the upper Ganges River Valley. In the third century BCE, the Mauryan king Ashoka became a Buddhist and promoted Buddhism, sending missionaries to southern India, the Himalayas, Sri Lanka, and Southeast Asia. Although the Mauryan Empire later collapsed and splintered into small kingdoms, Buddhism continued to flourish in northern India.

In the second century BCE, Chinese traders developed trade routes, now known collectively as the Silk Route, from China through Central Asia to the Mediterranean. Buddhism spread along the Silk Route and reached China in the first century CE and then spread across China by the fourth century CE, when a Chinese monk traveled to study at the great Buddhist monasteries in India for the first time.

In the sixth century CE, Turkish tribes won loose control of northern China, plundered the Silk Route, and suppressed Buddhism. However, by the end of the century, the Sui Dynasty came to power, reuniting China and restoring Buddhism.

In the seventh century CE, the Tang Dynasty came to power in southern China and expanded across Central Asia, allowing China to regain control of the Silk Route. Buddhism continued to gain popularity and imperial patronage. Meanwhile in northern India, the Gutpa Empire collapsed and a number of small kingdoms emerged. In some of these kingdoms Buddhism remained popular, while in others Hinduism regained popularity.

At the time, a number of small kingdoms and clan principalities existed in the valleys on each side of the Himalayas. Songtsen Gampo gained control of the Yarlung Valley on the northern side of the mountains and established the Tibetan Empire. King Songtsen Gampo conquered the Zhangzhung Kingdom in the west and secured Nepal, at that time a small kingdom in the Kathmandu Valley, as an ally. He also conquered the Azha region in the east and defeated the Chinese in battle. To strengthen his alliances, the king married Nepalese and Chinese princesses. Songtsen built a series of Buddhist temples, but it was not until the eighth century CE, when King Trisong

CENTRAL ASIA
CHINA
SILK ROUTE
Xian
Azha
TIBETAN REGION
Zhangzhung
HIMALAYAS
Lhasa
Ralung Monastery
Yarlung Valley
Nepal - Kathmandu Valley
Ganges River Valley
BHUTAN
INDIA
SOUTHEAST ASIA
Sri Lanka

Detsen made Buddhism the state religion, that it truly took root in Tibet. In his effort to establish Buddhism as the state religion, Trisong sought the assistance of several well-known Buddhist teachers, including Padmasambhava, who used his magical powers to subdue and convert local demons into Buddhist protective deities. In Bhutan, Padmasambhava is thought of as the second Buddha and is known as Guru Rinpoche (precious master). Over the centuries, temples have been built where he meditated, subdued a demon, and/or hid sacred texts for later generations to discover.

In the ninth century CE the Chinese emperor Wuzong, concerned by the amount of power and wealth Buddhist monks had gained in his realm, evicted the monks, confiscated their wealth, and destroyed their temples. In Tibet the Age of Fragmentation began, during which the empire collapsed, clans fought for control, and Buddhist monasteries were pillaged. Meanwhile, in northern India, Buddhism continued to flourish. Scholars from across Asia came to study at the great Buddhist monasteries there until the eleventh century, when Turks conquered the region and sacked the monasteries.

Buddhism takes root in Bhutan [2]

In the eleventh century, a new wave of Buddhist teachers revived Buddhism in Tibet. As various Buddhist schools emerged, factions within and between schools vied for power. Tibetan monks began to establish temples and monasteries in the border region that is now Bhutan; some were branch institutions established to expand a school, while others were splinter institutions established by monks fleeing power struggles.

At that time, a monk who founded a temple or monastery could develop secular in addition to religious authority and could establish a lineage to pass on his authority. If he had not yet taken a monk's vows, he could have a family and pass on his authority to a son. If he had taken a monk's vows, he could pass on his authority to a nephew or to a boy identified as his reincarnation. Sometimes, followers established a lineage after a monk's death. All of these were acceptable ways to continue a religious lineage and expand a Buddhist school.

In the early thirteenth century, Phajo Drukgom Zhigpo, a Tibetan Drukpa monk, established the first Drukpa temple and monastery in Bhutan. He passed on his authority to his four sons, who settled in different areas in order to expand the family lineage and the Drukpa school.

By the end of the sixteenth century, a number of Buddhist schools and associated leading families were established in Bhutan. Leading families from the Drukpa and other Tibetan Buddhist schools controlled western Bhutan, leading families from the Nyingmapa school and aristocratic families controlled central Bhutan, and various clans claiming descent from a ninth-century Tibetan prince controlled eastern Bhutan.

The Zhabdrung unifies Bhutan

In the early seventeenth century, Ngawang Namgyal, the grandson of the abbot of the Ralung Monastery in Tibet, was one of two boys identified as the reincarnation of the Drukpa school's great scholar. Ngawang Namgyal succeeded his grandfather as abbot, but the dispute about who was the great scholar's reincarnation continued. In 1616 Namgyal lost a legal battle related to the dispute and fled to western Bhutan. Over the following years, he traveled throughout western Bhutan gaining support of the leading Drukpa families. Although his initial goal was to take control of the Drukpa school in Tibet, in 1626 he decided instead to take control of the "Southern Land of Four Approaches," as Bhutan was then called, and " 'administer the Teaching according to the dual system [of religious and secular law].' "[3]

Ngawang Namgyal was a charismatic and skillful leader in both religious and secular affairs. By 1646 he had won over or defeated the other local Buddhist schools and had defeated Tibetan invasions, gaining control of western Bhutan. He became known as the Zhabdrung (at whose feet one submits) and was the overall religious and administrative leader of the region. He appointed a *je khenpo* (head of the monastic community) and a *desi* (chief administrator), and established religious and civil laws.

As the Zhabdrung and his followers conquered each district, they built a *dzong* to secure it and from which to administer religious and secular rule. The Zhabdrung died in 1651, but his death was kept secret, and by 1656 his administration had gained control of central and eastern Bhutan.

Bhutan survives internal struggles

While the Zhabdrung's dual system of government provided a consistent structure of governance and laws across the country, succession was a problem. Power struggles for control of the central government, and between the central and regional governments, became common. Eventually Bhutan's three *penlops* (regional governors) gained more power than the central government possessed, and by the late nineteenth century, the Paro Penlop controlled western Bhutan and the Trongsa Penlop controlled central and eastern Bhutan. In 1907, Ugyen Wangchuk, the Trongsa Penlop, secured enough power that he was made king, and a monarchy with a hereditary king replaced a theocracy with a reincarnated Zhabdrung, thus eliminating power struggles over succession. Gradually the country modernized, and in 2008 Bhutan became a democratic constitutional monarchy. Although Buddhism is no longer a part of the country's politics, it remains the foundation of Bhutan's principals and values, and the government continues to support Buddhism and Buddhist institutions.

Buddhism in Bhutan[4]

Buddhists believe that life and death are a continuum in which one's actions determine one's rebirth in an endless cycle of *samsara* (suffering). To be released from this cycle into the bliss of *nirvana* (enlightenment), one must understand the true nature of reality and practice moral conduct and meditation as described in the four noble truths and the noble eightfold path. The *four noble truths* state that (1) suffering exists, (2) the cause of suffering is ignorance, (3) ignorance can be eliminated, and (4) there exists a path to eliminate ignorance and attain enlightenment. This way is defined in the *noble eightfold path* as (1) right insight, (2) right aspiration, (3) right speech, (4) right conduct, (5) right livelihood, (6) right effort, (7) right mindfulness, and (8) right meditation attainment.[5]

The oldest forms of Buddhism survive within Theravada Buddhism (doctrine of the elders). Theravada is called Hinayana (inferior vehicle) by its detractors because it emphasizes individual enlightenment. Mahayana Buddhism (great vehicle) emphasizes enlightenment for all sentient beings. *Bodhisattvas*, followers of the Buddha who postpone their own enlightenment to help others achieve enlightenment, are key figures in Mahayana Buddhism. Vajrayana Buddhism, which is also known as Tantric Buddhism, includes rituals and visualizations considered powerful enough for one to achieve enlightenment in a single lifetime.[6]

The Drukpa school (Drukpa Kagyu school) and the Nyingmapa school are the primary Buddhist schools in Bhutan. Both are based in Mahayana and Vajrayana teaching. These schools recognize various forms of the Buddha, bodhisattvas, and historic figures who helped spread Buddhism in the region. Perhaps the best-known bodhisattva is Chenrezig (Avalokiteshvara in Sanskrit), the bodhisattva of compassion; and the best-known historical figure is Guru Rinpoche (Padmasambhava in Sanskrit), the great teacher who was renown for his magical powers that could subdue demons that were preventing the spread of Buddhism in the region.

Today Buddhism is an integral part of life in Bhutan. Many Bhutanese maintain a shrine at home; visit temples for blessings, rituals and festivals; make offerings; and help build and maintain religious structures. Elderly men and women can be found walking the circumambulation (*kora)* path around temples while reciting mantras and spinning prayer wheels. It is believed that all these acts bring merit and help one achieve a desirable rebirth on the path toward enlightenment. Bhutanese monks practice rituals and meditation with the aim of achieving a change in consciousness—including a different understanding of reality—that will lead to enlightenment. As novice monks progress through their training, some are selected for ritual training and others for philosophical training. Ultimately a few are selected for advanced visualization practice.

Perhaps the most visible icons of Bhutan and its Buddhist culture are its striking temples, monasteries, and dzongs. These buildings are both the centers of Bhutan's heritage and its hubs of contemporary life. The following sections provide an overview of Bhutan's Buddhist architecture; examples of each type of building; and a pictorial glossary of symbols used in building decoration.

Lhasa
CHINA
TIBETAN REGION
Yarlung Valley
Ralung Monastery
H I M A L A Y A S
Mo River
Pho River
Thimphu River
Paro River
Mangde River
Bumthang River
Karu River
Kulong River
Punakha
Thimphu
Paro
Trongsa
Jakar, Chokhor Valley
Phobjikha Valley
Chhume Valley
Torsa River
Ha River
Puna Tsang River
BHUTAN
Gamri River
Trashigang
Drongmo River

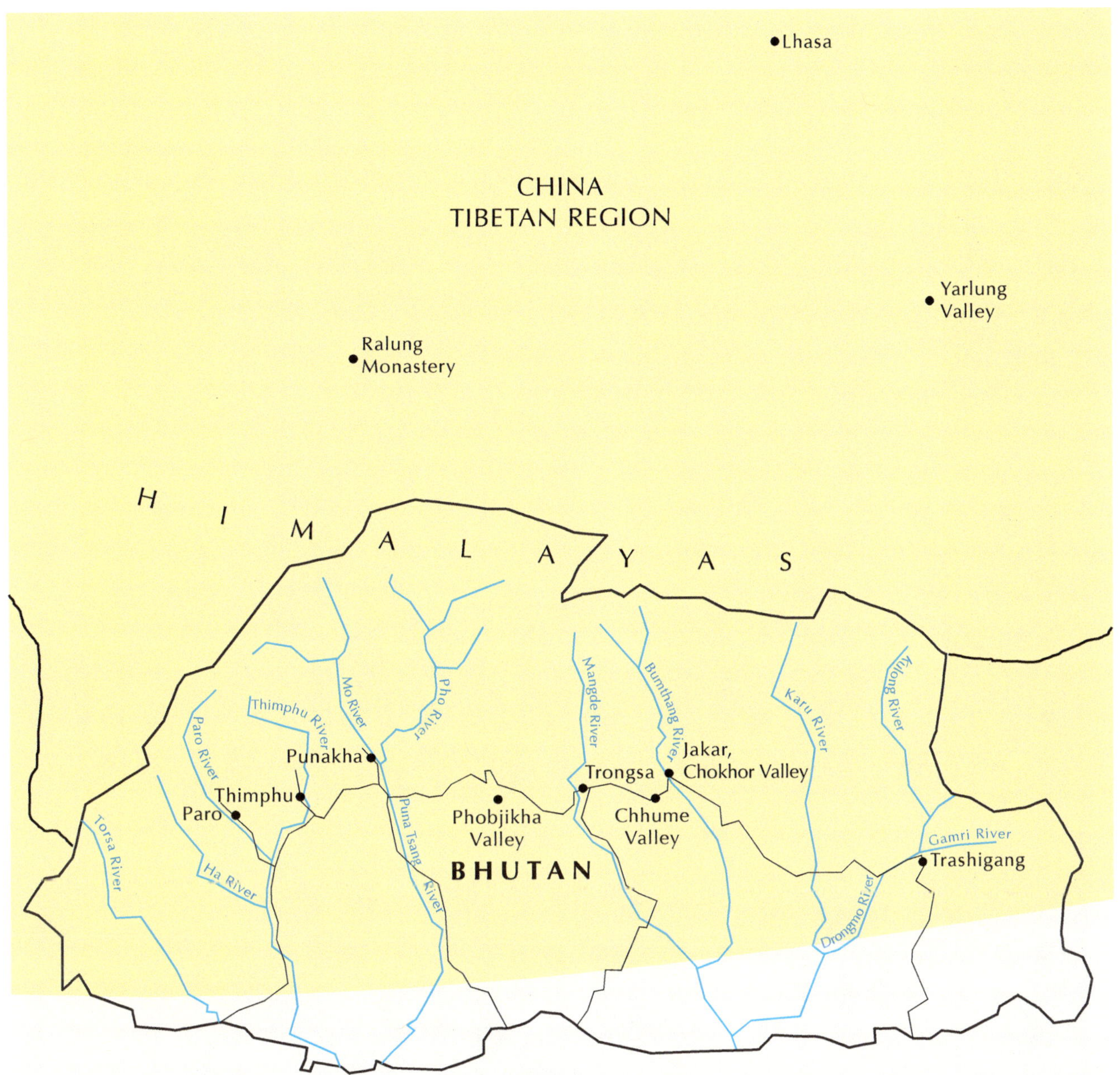

INDIA

ARCHITECTURAL OVERVIEW

Punakha Dzong

Bhutan's Buddhist architecture has a distinct character, which evolved to suit its environment, needs, and traditions. Each structure is built using local materials and following traditional practices adapted for each circumstance. The result is a consistent—but not formulaic—architectural style. Each building is readily recognizable both as Bhutanese and as unique.

The following architectural overview describes Indian and Tibetan precedents that influenced Bhutan's Buddhist architecture as well as characteristics typical of Bhutan's temples, monasteries, and dzongs—the fortresses built by the Zhabdrung and his followers while unifying Bhutan as a Buddhist state.

Indian precedents

Buddhist architecture emerged along with Buddhism in northern India. While the first Buddhist monks were wandering ascetics with no permanent temples or residences, monks soon began to settle in temples and monasteries.

Early Indian Buddhist temples such as Ajanta Cave 26 (upper right) were carved into cliffs, and are typically rectangular with a round end and have an inner prayer hall, a colonnade and an outer ambulatory (walkway). An entry door with a large window above it is located opposite the round end, where a stupa (symbol of the Buddha), or a statue of the Buddha is the focus of worship.

Indian monasteries are typically square, with small cells lining the inside of the exterior walls. An entry porch is located opposite a shrine centered on one wall. By the second century CE, Indian temples and monasteries had typical features including stepped door frames, windows with scallop-shaped heads, and columns with bracket tops.

Tibetan precedents

The first Tibetan Buddhist temples, built in the seventh century CE, have layouts and details similar to Indian temples and monasteries. By the eleventh century CE, however, with Buddhism gaining popularity, Tibetan temples and monasteries had begun to change to suit local religious and building practices.[7]

By the fourteenth century Tibetan Buddhist architecture had evolved. Freestanding temples are typically larger and do not have an ambulatory. Temples built as part of a monastery are typically two-story buildings with an assembly hall and a sanctum on the first floor, and sitting rooms on the second. The entry facade looks south and has a first-floor entry porch and a second-floor balcony window that provides light and warmth for the senior monks' sitting room. Some temples have a mandala (sacred diagram) shaped plan in which an assembly hall and sanctum are flanked by side rooms. Despite such changes, some features adopted from Indian architecture, such as stepped door frames, scalloped-shaped windows, and bracket topped columns, were retained.

Bhutan's Buddhist architecture

The basic layout, materials, and features of Bhutanese temples, monasteries, and dzongs are similar to their Tibetan precedents, but Bhutan's buildings have a different character. Both Bhutanese and Tibetan buildings are built using a combination of stone or rammed (compressed) earth and wood; however, since

Ajanta Cave 26, **Indian Temple**
Photograph by Dey.sandip via Wikimedia Commons

Lalitgiri, **Indian Monastery**
Photograph by Daniel Limma via Wikimedia Commons

Jokhang, **Tibetan Temple**
Photograph by Cathy Ann Taylor, Catarra LLC

Samye Monastery, **Tibetan Monastery**
Photograph by Cathy Ann Taylor, Catarra LLC

Kurje Lhakhang, **Bhutanese Temple**

Gangte Goemba, **Bhutanese Monastery**

there is more precipitation in Bhutan, its buildings have sloped rather than flat roofs to allow rain and snow to shed, and since there are more trees in Bhutan, its buildings have more woodwork. In addition, Bhutanese woodwork is more elaborate and richly decorated. The sloped roofs and the more extensive and elaborate woodwork and decoration give Bhutan's buildings a distinct character.

Temples

Bhutan's temples are known as deity palaces (*lhakhangs*). The earliest temples such as Jampa Lhakhang (upper right and pp. 24–27), are small, one-story structures with a taller sanctuary surrounded by a lower east-facing entry and ambulatory. By the fourteenth century freestanding temples, such as Changangkha Lhakhang (pp. 28–31), were being built; these are larger, one- or two-story buildings with a square or rectangular plan and a south-facing entry but no ambulatory. Temples built as part of a monastery, such as the one at the Gangte Goemba (lower right and pp. 46–49), are large two- or three-story buildings with a square, rectangular, or mandala-shaped plan and an entry porch (*gorikha*).

Temple interiors can be one space with statues, an offering table, and floor space; or divided into a sanctum with statues and an offering table and an assembly hall with a seat for the lama and floor space for the monks to sit. If the temple has multiple stories, it can have several sanctuaries. Thus, one temple building can house multiple sanctuaries, each called a temple and named for its primary figure of worship.

Most temples have a sanctuary for fierce protective deities (*goenkhang*) which is located in a side room within the main sanctuary or, in larger temple buildings, in a separate sanctuary.

Monasteries

Bhutan's monasteries (*goembas*) typically have a temple building surrounded by buildings for the monk community. As Françoise Pommaret describes in her book *Bhutan—Himalayan Mountain Kingdom*, some monasteries are courtyard buildings with a temple building in the middle, and monastic housing and community spaces lining the inside of courtyard walls, while other monasteries are simply a cluster of buildings.[8] It is likely such clusters resulted from the constraints of topography and/or the addition of buildings as needed.

Temples and monasteries were often built on sacred sites where a famous Buddhist teacher had meditated, suppressed a local demon, had a vision, or recognized the fulfillment of a prophecy. Some of these sites were prominent locations in, or overlooking valleys, while others were remote mountain locations.

Dzongs

Most of Bhutan's dzongs were built in the seventeenth century by the Zhabdrung and his followers while unifying Bhutan. The dzongs were built to secure and protect each district, house a monastic community and administer the district according to a dual system of religious and secular law.

Dzongs were built on sites that were prominent, strategic and sacred. Typically a dzong is located on a highly visible spur or ridge that has a good view of the surroundings and has

Jampa Lhakhang

Gangte Goemba

access to water, but whose topography would make the dzong difficult to attack. A few dzongs are located in valleys along rivers but away from surrounding high ground that could be used by attackers. Given their prominent locations, a number of dzong sites were first occupied by a temple, monastery, or family seat and later given to or secured by the Zhabdrung and his followers.

Dzongs are two- to four-story courtyard buildings with a tower. The courtyard (*dochey*), or courtyards in larger dzongs, are lined with rooms for administrative and monastic uses, and the tower (*utse*) has several temples and apartments for senior monks. Dzongs located on a wide spur or in a valley typically have a more regular layout, with the tower located inside the exterior wall, while dzongs located on a narrow spur or ridge typically have a less regular layout—which steps and turns with the topography—and the tower integrated into the exterior wall.

Dzongs have a number of defensive features, some of which were adopted from Tibetan stone towers, civil fortresses, and fortified monasteries.[9] The exterior walls are massive, with a few small openings—sometimes only narrow slots from which attackers could be shot—on the lowest level. The top of the walls do not extend all the way to the underside of the roof leaving an open-air attic that could be used as a battery in case of attack. Most dzongs originally had one entry, with a stout wood door. Often the entry and courtyard are raised above grade (ground level) and were originally reached using a ladder, which could be removed for security. When the courtyard was raised, the space below it was used to store food and other supplies. Like the outer dzong structure, the tower has massive walls with few openings on the lower levels, and sometimes the lowest floor is raised above the courtyard and was originally reached by a removable ladder. In case of attack, the courtyard could house troops and/or locals, and the tower could be used as an inner citadel. In addition, some dzongs have outer defense walls, watchtowers, and/or a protected passage to a spring or river.

Although no longer defensive structures, dzongs still house government offices and monk communities, and they remain the political, religious, and cultural hub of each district. Typically, the government offices are located near the entry, and the monastic community is located in a second courtyard, if there is one.

Typical Building Characteristics

As Dorji Yangki describes in an article on Bhutan's sacred architecture, a building's height, form, roof design, color, and decoration reflect its hierarchy or entitlement (*thobthang*). Thus, temples, monasteries, and dzongs often occupy a prominent site and are the tallest and most elaborate buildings in Bhutan.[10] In addition, the buildings are built with great skill and care under the direction of a master carpenter, who follows traditional design and construction practices. The combination of location, design, and artisanship give the buildings a majestic presence.

Typically, the exterior walls are thick stone structures that taper from the base to the top in order to improve their stability and resistance to earthquakes. The inside faces are coated with clay to protect the interior spaces

Simtokha Dzong

Punakha Dzong

from wind and rain. The lower levels have a few smaller openings while the upper levels have more larger openings. The walls, which are whitewashed, have a red band near the top. The whitewash symbolizes purity and the red band (*kemar*) signifies the fact that the building houses religious functions. In Tibet, the kemar is usually a rammed-earth parapet built above a flat roof, while in Bhutan it is stone like the rest of the wall and is usually demarcated at the top and bottom by a row of decorative wood joist ends.

The wood roof structures are set above the walls, are sloped, and project out. The gap between the walls and the roof can be fairly large, and can function as an open attic used to dry and store food, or in the case of dzongs as a vantage point in battle. The roof slope and projection provide protection from rain and snow. The roofing was originally wood shingles held down with stones, but now is typically metal. Often, roofs are layered and topped with ornaments, indicating the building's entitlement. As described in Bhutan's Department of Urban Housing's *Traditional Architecture Guide*, temples that house relics are topped with a gold finial (*sertog*) mounted on a wood lantern roof structure (*jabzhi*). Together, the sertog and jabzhi resemble a stupa, which symbolizes the Buddha. Temples with a large number of sacred texts have a gold victory banner (*gyaltshen*) which represents the victory of the Buddha's teaching over ignorance.[11]

The wood entry door (*mago*) typically has a stepped door frame reminiscent of an Indian entry door. Often the Bhutanese entry door is decorated with a large painted dharma wheel, a symbol of the Buddha's teaching, and has a raised threshold to keep evil spirits out.

Large wood-framed elements (*rabsels*) can be set flush with masonry walls or project out as balcony windows or arcades. A rabsel can be a single story with only a few openings, or several stories with many openings. Small windows (*geykars*) and larger windows with several openings (*payabs*) often can be found below and/or between rabsels.

Arcades and porches are supported by traditional columns. Each column (*kachen*) has a tapered post and an elongated top bracket (*zhu*). A column can be simply formed and painted or can be elaborately formed, carved, and painted. Although the decoration differs, Bhutanese columns such as those at Punakha Dzong (p. 21) are reminiscent of Indian columns such as those at Ajanta Cave 26 (p.13).

While the masonry is simple, the woodwork is complex and is decorated with carved and/or painted motifs, script, animals, and figures; many of which are Buddhist symbols. The integration of woodworking, carving, and painting into Buddhist building design is not unique to Bhutan, but some of the details and the extent to which decoration is integrated into the building exteriors are unique. As Françoise Pommaret describes in her book *Bhutan—Himalayan Mountain Kingdom*, woodworking, carving and painting follow strict rules of composition, proportion, and iconography. Building decoration, like all traditional arts in Bhutan, is religious and its origin anonymous; it is undertaken as religious work rather than as a means of personal expression.[12] As with the design of the buildings themselves, the decoration of the woodwork is not formulaic. While some of the symbols used and

Jakar Dzong

where they are incorporated are fairly typical, the decoration of each building is unique. The Symbols section (pp. 85–101) provides a brief introduction to Buddhist symbols as well as examples and descriptions of symbols commonly used in building decoration.

Conclusion

Bhutan's sacred architecture has a distinct and striking character that evolved to suit Bhutan's natural environment, functional needs, and Buddhist traditions. Each temple, monastery and dzong is sited and built using local materials and following traditional practices adapted for each circumstance. Traditional construction and decoration practices give the buildings consistency, yet the need for and acceptance of adaptability means each building was located and built to suit specific conditions and needs. Also, in keeping with the Buddhist belief in impermanence and the demands of ongoing use, changes are expected and regularly undertaken. Most buildings have been renovated and expanded a number of times since they were first built. Renovations are done to repair deterioration from the harsh climate and damage from earthquakes, fires, and—until modern times—attacks. Expansions are done to accommodate growing needs and for patronage. Today, Bhutan's sacred buildings are larger, more complex, and more extensively and elaborately decorated. The new blends with the old, however, because the basic forms, materials, details, and decoration adhere to traditional practices that have evolved slowly. The result of this evolution is architecture that both is traditional and benefits from the vibrancy of ongoing adaptation and use.

The following sections provide examples of Bhutan's temples, monasteries, and dzongs. The examples were selected both for their individual qualities and to illustrate the characteristics in the country's Buddhist architecture.

TEMPLES

• Taktshang Pelphug

Jampa Lhakhang

According to legend, in the seventh-century CE, Tibetan king Songtsen Gampo built 108 temples to subdue the Earth Goddess of Tibet, a demoness that dominated the region and was preventing the spread of Buddhism. At the time, Bhutan was a borderland of Tibet, and Jampa Lhakhang was built in order to pin down the demoness's left knee. Today it is popular both as a local temple and a pilgrimage destination.

Jampa Lhakhang (temple of the future Buddha) is located on the west side of the Chokhor Valley in central Bhutan. The original building, shown below, is a small, square one-story structure with a tall sanctuary surrounded by a low ambulatory (walkway). Both the sanctuary and the ambulatory have traditional whitewashed stone walls with a red band and simple shed roofs. The entry facade looks east and has a large central window and a side entry door. Jampa Lhakhang's configuration and orientation is typical of temples built in the region during the seventh through the ninth centuries CE.

Over the centuries additional buildings have been built around the original Jampa Lhakhang, and today it is a small courtyard complex. The original temple forms the west side of the courtyard, and three other temple buildings and a residential building form the other sides.

The complex has the wonderful feel of an ancient but active temple. Monks chant prayers; elderly practitioners spend their days walking clockwise around the complex, spinning prayer wheels, and reciting mantras; and practitioners from across Bhutan gather for an annual festival.

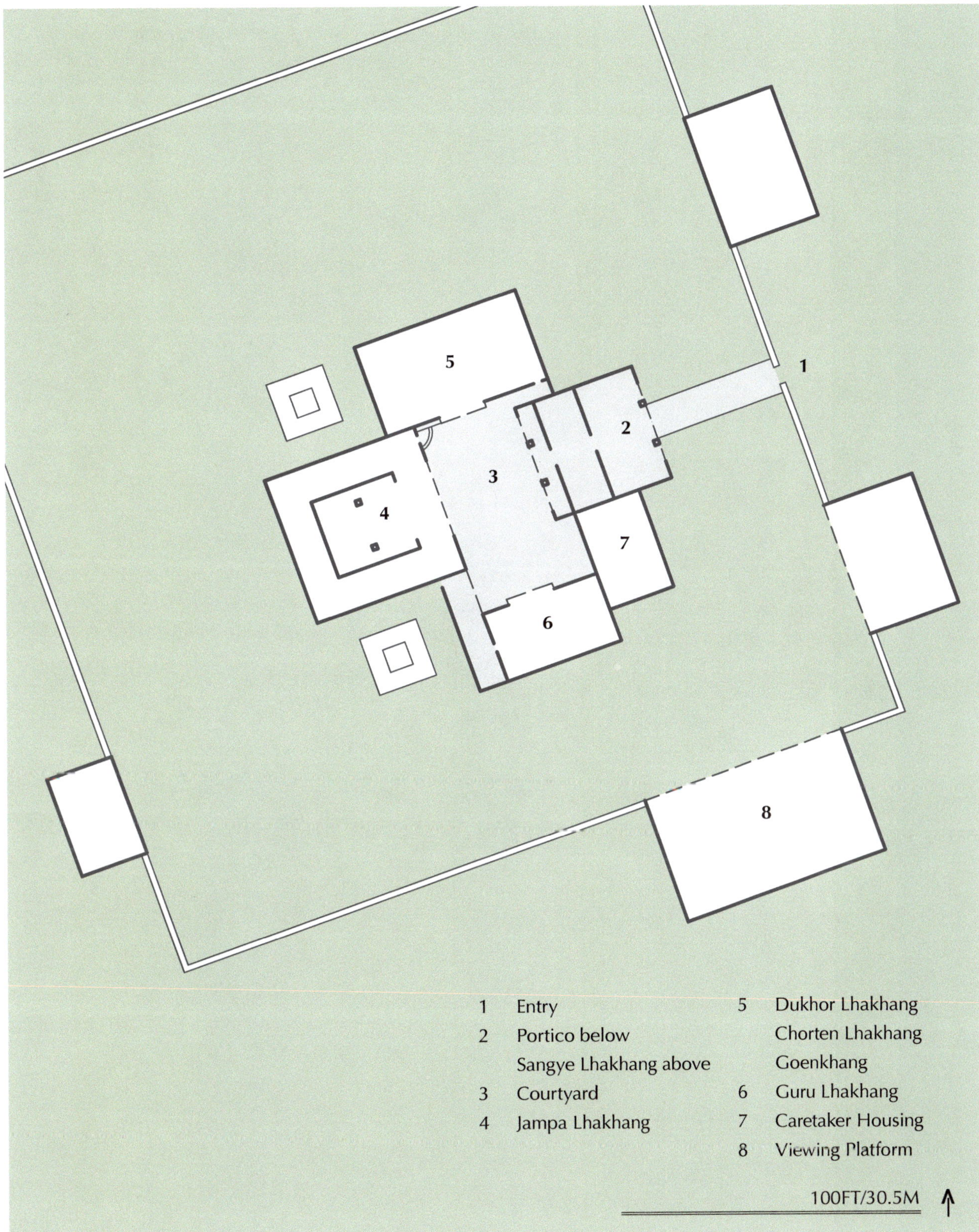
1
2
3
4
5
6
7
8
1 Entry
2 Portico below
Sangye Lhakhang above
3 Courtyard
4 Jampa Lhakhang
5 Dukhor Lhakhang
Chorten Lhakhang
Goenkhang
6 Guru Lhakhang
7 Caretaker Housing
8 Viewing Platform
100FT/30.5M

The entry gate, on the left, leads to the east-wing portico and the courtyard beyond. The portico, with its traditional columns and prayer wheels, is a variation of a temple entry porch. The mantra *om mani padme hum* is carved in the lintel above the portico. Mani means jewel, which symbolizes method, and padme means lotus, which symbolizes wisdom. Thus, the mantra, described in more detail on page 94, refers to ultimate truth and the means to realize it.

Changangkha Lhakhang

In the thirteenth century the Tibetan Buddhist monk Phajo Drukgom Zhigpo established the Drukpa school in Bhutan. After founding a temple and monastery, he passed his authority on to his four sons in order to expand the family lineage and the Drukpa school. His son Nyima settled in the Thimphu Valley and established a leading family known as the Changangkha Shelgno, which built Changangkha Lhakhang in the fourteenth century. It is one of the oldest temples in the valley and is a popular temple to which to bring a newborn for naming.

Changangkha Lhakhang is located on a spur on the west side of the Thimphu Valley. The temple building is a tall one-story structure with a square plan. Prayer wheels wrap the building, creating a circumambulation *(kora)* path around the temple. Its main facade looks south and has a large central window, flanked by two smaller windows. This configuration with an exterior kora path rather than interior ambulatory, and a south rather than an east orientation became common in the region in the fourteen century.

Today the temple fronts a small courtyard and is surrounded by buildings that were built later, including a residential wing for caretakers on the east side of the courtyard and a temple for fierce protective deities (*goenkhang*) on the south side of the courtyard.

Set on a stone plinth (base) overlooking the valley, Changangkha Lhakhang has a slightly removed and contemplative feel, though a steady stream of locals visiting as part of their daily routine gives it a quiet hum of activity.

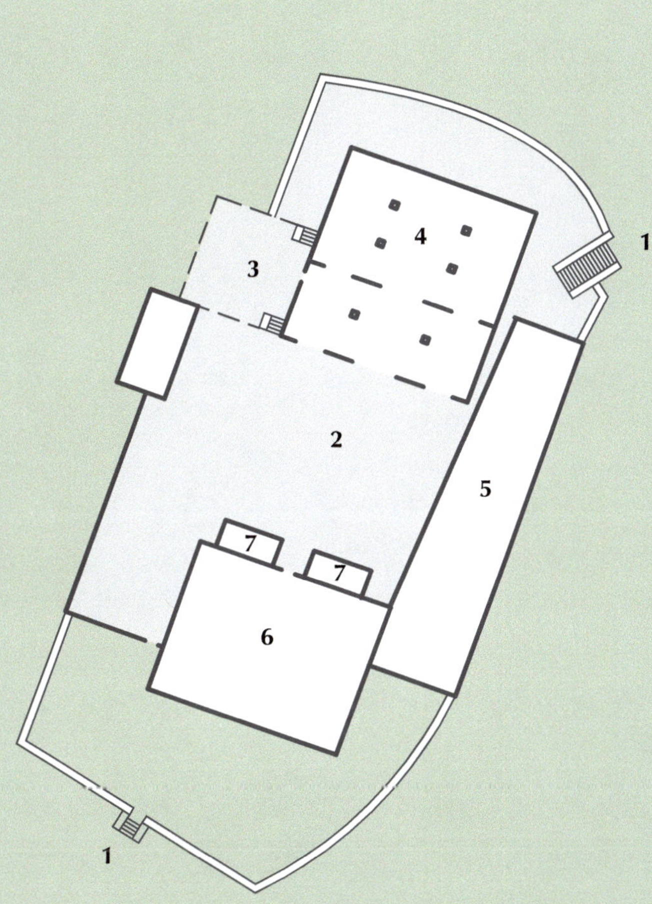

1 Entry
2 Courtyard
3 Porch
4 Temple
5 Caretaker Housing
6 Goenkhang
7 Butter Lamp

100FT/30.5M

Prayer wheels, housed in a traditional wood structure set on a stone base, wrap the temple exterior. The structure features a slate roof, a wood cornice, and framed openings with scallop-shaped heads, and it is lined with slate carvings. Each prayer wheel has a metal cylinder with a prayer on it, a roll of paper with the prayer written multiple times inside it, and a wood handle to spin it.

Practitioners, such as the woman shown on the right, walk the kora path around the temple while reciting prayers and spinning the prayer wheels. The simple act of spinning a prayer wheel is said to benefit the practitioner by focusing the body, speech, and mind, and to benefit all sentient beings by spreading the prayer.[13] And the ritual of walking the kora path is believed to bring merit and help the practitioner achieve a desirable rebirth on the path toward enlightenment.

Kurje Lhakhang

It is said that a king who ruled in central Bhutan in the eighth century CE, distraught after his son had been killed in battle, forgot to worship his personal deity. The deity became angry and withdrew the king's vital principle. Fearing that the king would die, his ministers sought help from Guru Rinpoche (Padmasambhava), the great Indian Buddhist teacher renowned for his magical powers. When Guru Rinpoche arrived, he mediated and then, using magic, seized the deity and forced it to return the king's vital principle and become a protective deity of Buddhism. Kurje Lhakhang (temple of the body imprint) was built where Guru Rinpoche left his imprint while meditating before subduing the deity. It is one of the most sacred sites in Bhutan.

Kurje Lhakhang is located on the west side of the Chokhor Valley in central Bhutan. Today the complex has three temple buildings and several stupas (*chortens*), butter lamp pavilions, and residential buildings, all enclosed by 108 chortens. Guru Lhakhang, on the right in the image below, was built in 1652; Sampa Lhundrup Lhakhang, in the middle, was built in 1900, and Khenlop Choesum Lhakhang, on the left, was built in 1990.

With its three large temple buildings set in a row along the base of a mountain and surrounded by an enclosure of chortens, the complex has a formal sacred presence.

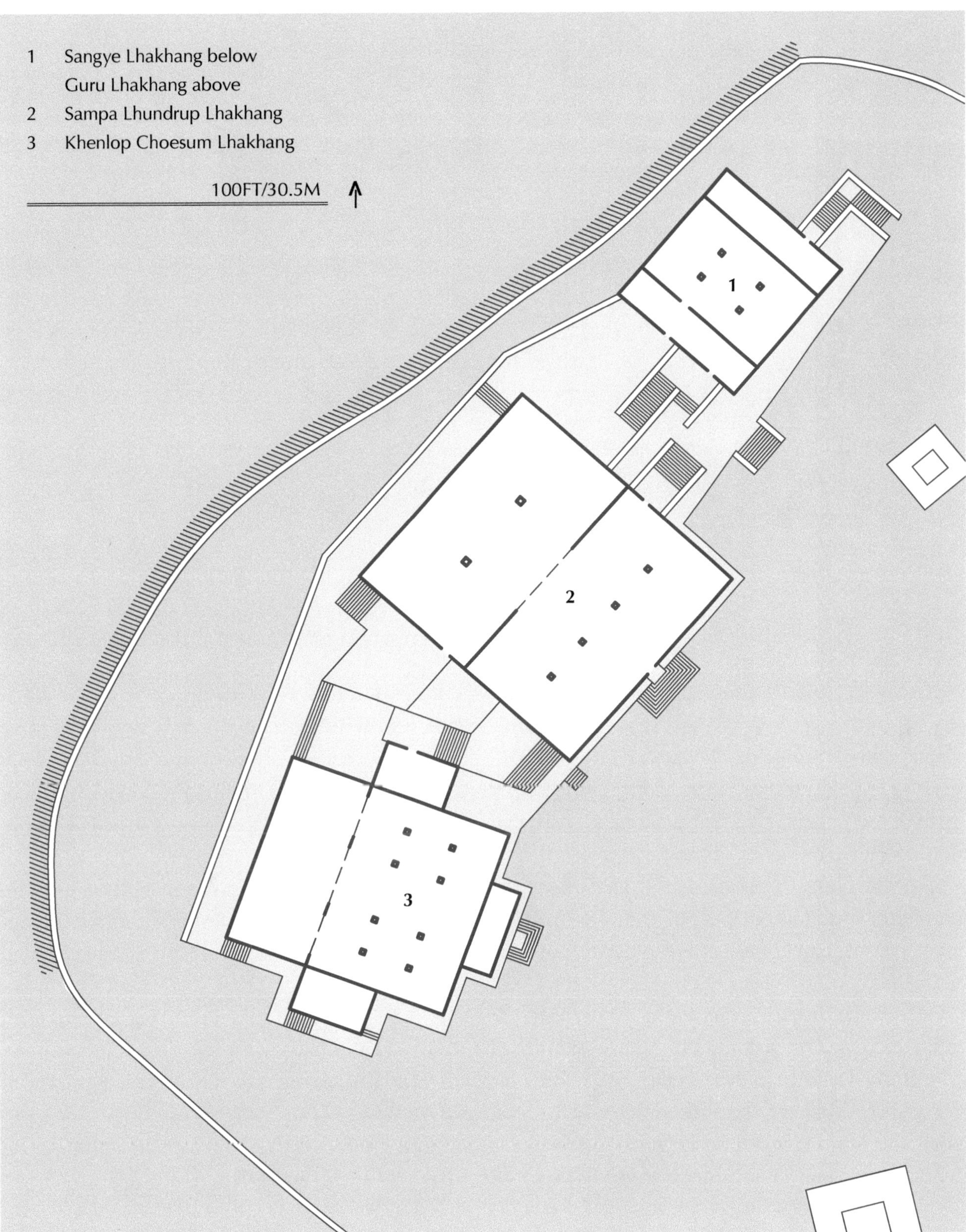
1 Sangye Lhakhang below
Guru Lhakhang above
2 Sampa Lhundrup Lhakhang
3 Khenlop Choesum Lhakhang
100FT/30.5M
1
2
3

While all three temple buildings are three-stories tall and have a symmetrically composed facade, each is different:

Guru Lhakhang, shown above, was built in the form of a tower; its wings were added later. The original building had a compact footprint with small windows on the first floor and larger balcony windows on the upper floors. The first floor was raised above grade and was likely reached by a ladder, which could be pulled up in case of attack. This configuration, which probably evolved from early Tibetan stone towers, can be found in smaller freestanding temples, larger monastery temples, and dzong towers.

Sampa Lhundrup Lhakhang, shown on the upper right, is a rectangular structure with its main entry and temple located on the second floor reached by an exterior stair. Half of the second floor is an assembly hall, and the other half a two-story sanctum housing a grand statue of Guru Rinpoche.

Khenlop Choesum Lhakhang, shown on the lower right, is a mandala-shaped structure with its main entry and accompanying porch on the front facade and secondary entries in the wings.

Sampa Lhundrup Lhakhang and Khenlop Choesum Lhakhang are larger and have more elaborate woodwork than the older Guru Lhakhang, yet even though they were built when defense was no longer a concern, they follow the traditional practice of having smaller windows on the first floor and increasingly larger balcony windows on the upper floors.

Taktshang Pelphug

According to legend, in the eighth century CE, the great Indian Buddhist teacher Guru Rinpoche (Padmasambhava) traveled throughout the Himalayas using his magical powers to subdue demons that were preventing the spread of Buddhism. It is said that he flew on the back of a tigress to a cliff above the Paro Valley, where he meditated in a cave and then subdued a local demon and converted the valley's inhabitants to Buddhism. Over the centuries, many Buddhist teachers have visited and meditated in the cave, and a number of temples have been built on the cliff.

Taktshang Pelphug was built over the cave where Guru Rinpoche meditated. The original temple was replaced with a temple complex in the seventeenth century, and the complex was most recently renovated in 1998, after a fire. Taktshang means tiger's lair and Pelphug means Pelki's cave—a reference to one of Guru Rinpoche disciples who visited the site. Today it is known in the west as Tiger's Nest and is one of the most sacred and popular pilgrimage destinations in Bhutan.

Taktshang Pelphug is a series of temple buildings configured and oriented to fit the available ledge space; they are connected by stairs, passages, and walks that wind through the complex. The result is a remarkable temple complex magically perched on the cliff renown for its sacred history.

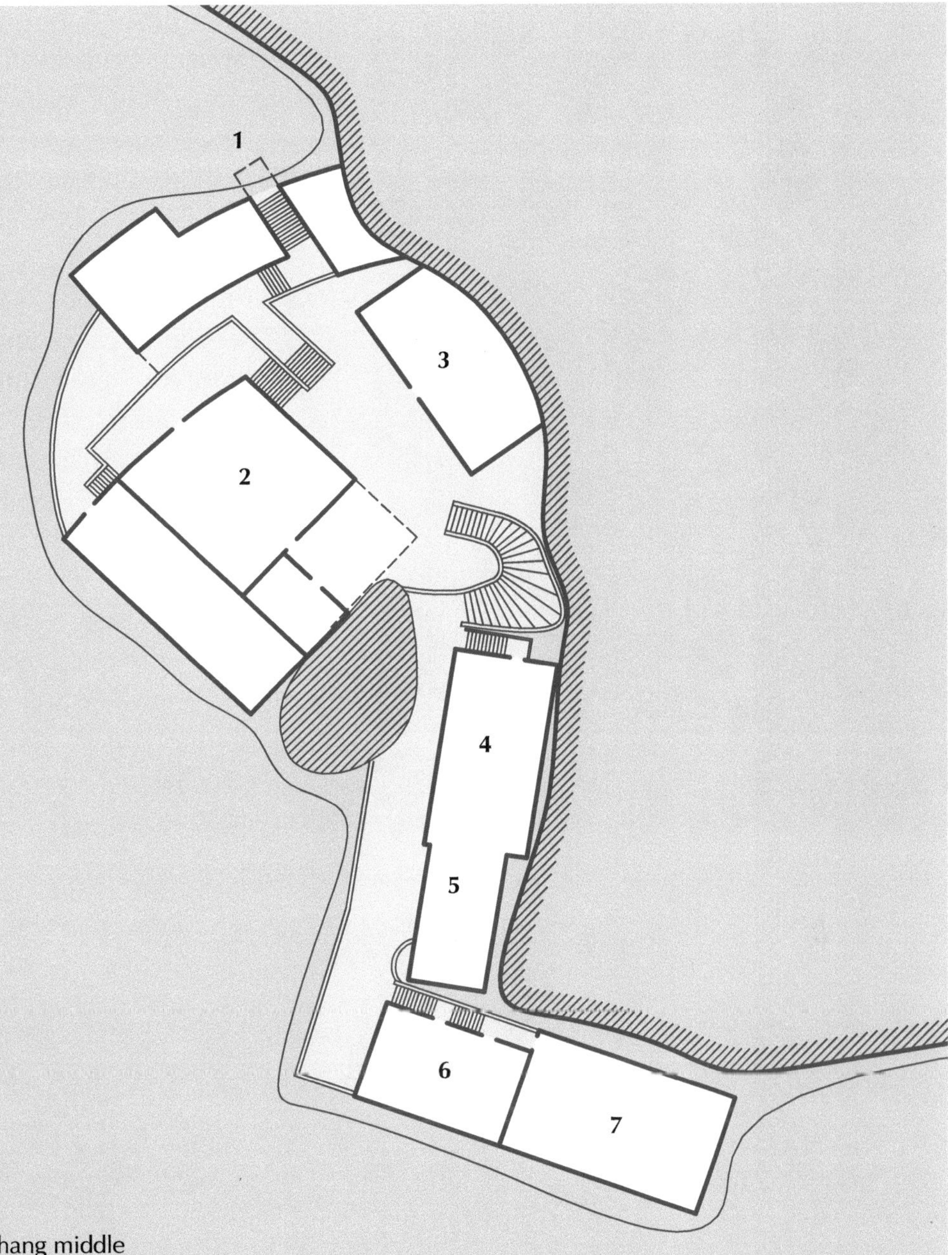

1 Entry
2 Dubkhang below
Guru Sungjem Lhakhang middle
Guru Tsengey Lhakhang above
3 Langchen Pelgye Tsengay Lhakhang
4 Drolo Lhakhang
5 Butter Lamp
6 Namsey Lhakhang
7 Tshepamed Lhakhang

100FT/30.5M

Although each building in the complex has a different form and orientation, all are easily recognizable as Bhutanese temples. The buildings have tapered, whitewashed stone walls with a red band near the top and sloped roofs topped with wood roof lanterns and gold ornaments. The red band (*kemar*) indicates that the building houses religious functions.

The roof design indicates each building's significance. A gold finial (*sertog*) mounted on a wood lantern structure (*jabzhi*) can only be mounted on temples that house relics. A tiered jabzhi is reserved for temples that house the most sacred relics.[11] Accordingly, the temple built over the cave where Guru Rinpoche meditated, shown in the foreground on the right, has a sertog on a tiered jabzhi. While much of Bhutan's Buddhist architecture is derived from Indian and Tibetan precedents, the roof designs are likely to have been influenced by Chinese precedents.

MONASTERIES

Tango Goemba

Tango Goemba

In the thirteenth century, the Tibetan monk Phajo Drukgom Zhigpo came to Bhutan to spread the Drukpa teaching throughout the land. It is said that, when he arrived in the Thimphu Valley, he heard neighing and saw the deity Tamdrin (Hayagriva in Sanskrit) on the mountainside. The deity told him to introduce the Drukpa school through his lineage. Phajo built a residence where he saw the deity, taught his sons the Drukpa teaching, and sent them to different areas to spread the teaching and family lineage.

Tango Goemba (horse head monastery) is located on a mountain at the north end of the Thimphu Valley. Tenzin Rabgye, the Zhabdrung's heir and Bhutan's fourth desi replaced Phajo's residence with a temple in the seventeenth century. Today Tango Goemba houses a monastic university and the residence of Tri Rinpoche, the reincarnation of Tenzin Rabgye.

Tango Goemba is a beautifully sited and designed monastery with a three-story temple building and a small courtyard nestled into a mountainside and enclosed within a one-story building that extends out from the mountain and has two lower levels. The elegant curve of the courtyard building complements the facets of the mandala-shaped tower.

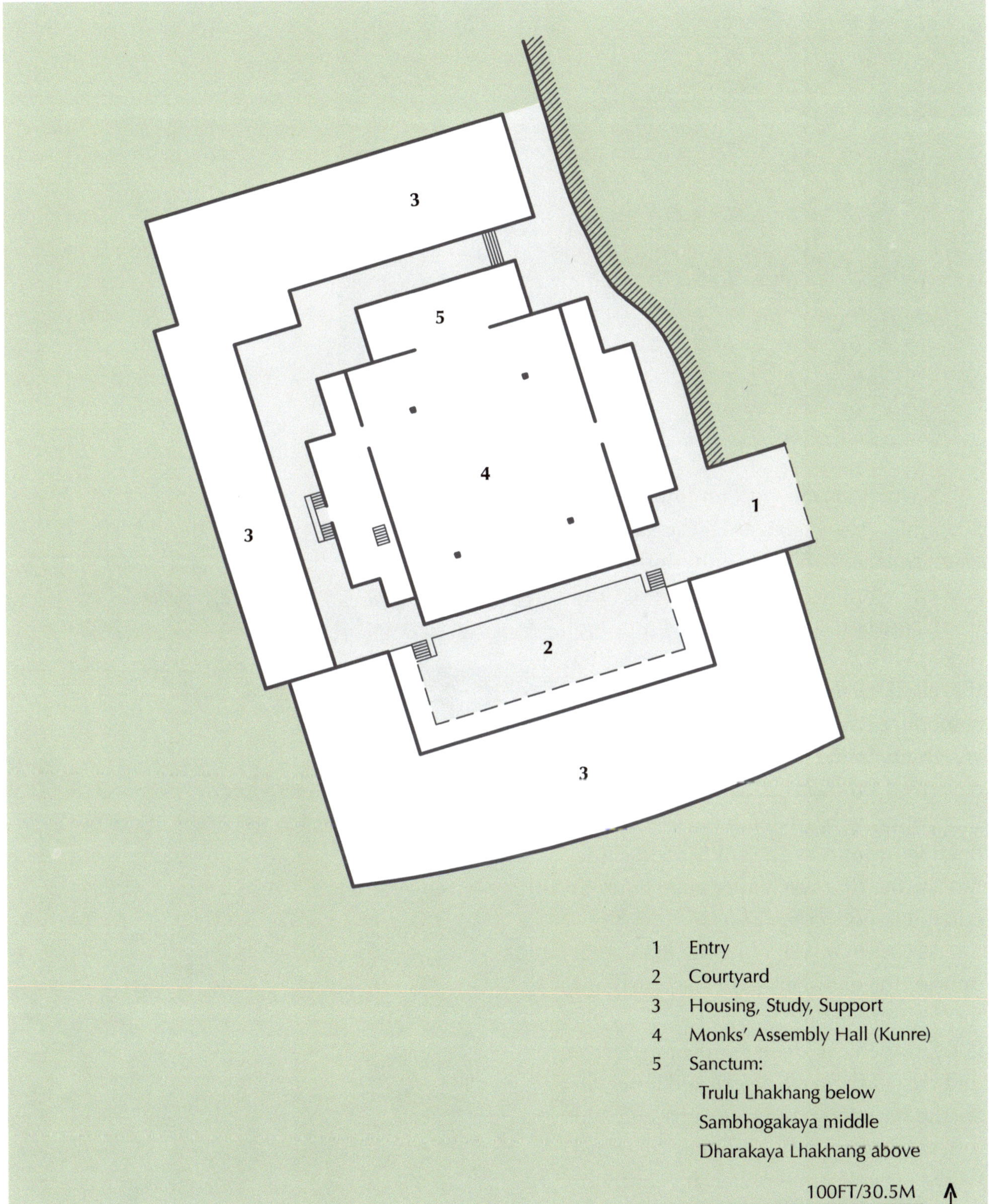
3
5
4
1
3
2
3
1 Entry
2 Courtyard
3 Housing, Study, Support
4 Monks' Assembly Hall (Kunre)
5 Sanctum:
Trulu Lhakhang below
Sambhogakaya middle
Dharakaya Lhakhang above
100FT/30.5M

A wood arcade with an unusual design lines the courtyard. The arcade's framework is filled with intricately carved window openings above and fixed panels below. The panels are decorated with Buddhist symbols, including the eight auspicious substances, which symbolize the noble eightfold path to enlightenment. Each of these substances, described on pages 90 and 91, is shown in an offering bowl and has a silk ribbon floating around it. The silk ribbon signifies the Buddha's brilliance and ability to adapt to any circumstance.

As shown on the right, the monks set up a shrine and shelters in the courtyard for their university graduation. They eagerly waited for their families to arrive and served them tea before and lunch after the ceremony. The ceremony entailed a presentation of the monks' collective work—a new book—rather than individual diplomas.

Gangte Goemba

Pema Lingpa was born in the fifteenth century into a leading religious family in central Bhutan. He was a Nyingmapa teacher and one of the great treasure discoverers (*tertons*), who found texts and relics that Guru Rinpoche (Padmasambhava) had hidden in the eighth century CE. His descendants continued his lineage and teaching, and one of his grandsons founded Gangte Goemba in the seventeenth century. Today Gangte Goemba is the largest Nyingmapa monastery in Bhutan and has about thirty five associated meditation and learning centers.[14]

Officially known as Gangteng Sangngak Chöling Goemba (monastery near a summit for teaching the dharma), this monastery is located on a hill overlooking the Phobjikha Valley in western Bhutan.

Gangte Goemba has a large and elaborate three-story temple building and vast courtyard enclosed by simple one- and two-story buildings. The temple building has a mandala-shaped plan with a main, south-facing entry and secondary east- and west-facing entries. The interior is an impressive wood structure with three levels of balconies wrapping around a central opening. The main temple is on the first floor, and several temples and apartments are on the second and third floors.

With its hilltop location and grand temple building rising high above the surrounding village, Gangte Goemba has a prominent presence.

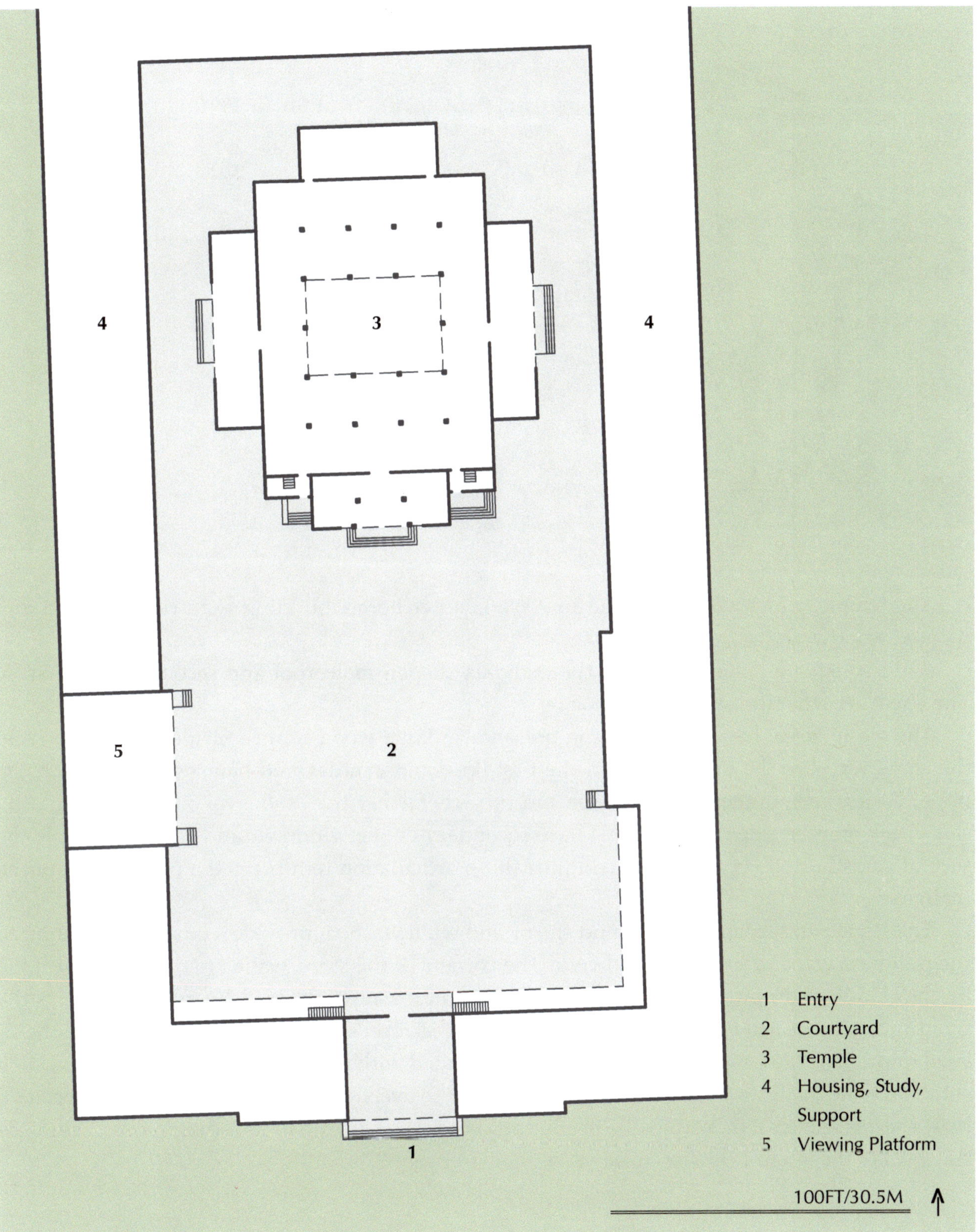
4
3
4
5
2
1
1 Entry
2 Courtyard
3 Temple
4 Housing, Study, Support
5 Viewing Platform
100FT/30.5M

The temple, which was renovated in 2008, is an elaborate building with richly carved and painted woodwork.

A tiered square lantern is set on the mandala-shaped main roof and secondary overhangs. The effect is both impressive and imposing.

The main facade has a commanding presence. A large wood framed element (*rabsel*) set into the stone wall has the main entry on the first floor and cantilevered balcony windows on the upper floors. Each higher level is wider and projects farther than the level below. The building steps back on each side; the first steps have secondary doors, windows, and balconies, while the second steps have no openings. This diminishing articulation reinforces the prominence of the main entry.

The stone walls, coated with a mud slurry and whitewashed, provide a crisp counterpoint to the richly carved and painted woodwork. The corners of the stone walls are decorated with the mythical king of the birds and snow lions. The mythical king of the birds (*garuda*) represents the wrathful form of Guru Rinpoche. The snow lion (*singye*) represents the joyful and fearless enlightened mind. The lintel above the entry porch is decorated with the *seven jewels of royal power,* which symbolize the qualities a practitioner needs in order to overcome all obstacles and be reborn as a *chakravartin* (universal monarch) like the Buddha who is considered to be the supreme Chakravartin. Each of these jewels is shown and described on pages 92 and 93.

Nyimalung Goemba

Nyimalung Goemba was founded in 1934 by a Tibetan Nyingmapa monk with the support of a local Bhutanese administrator.

Although commonly called Nyimalung Goemba (temple of sun and wind), the monastery is officially named Shaydrup Darjay Choling (a place for studying arts, literature and meditation and spreading Buddha's teaching).[15]

Nyimalung Goemba is located in a remote portion of the Chhume Valley in central Bhutan. Built in an era when fortifications were no longer needed, the main temple building fronts an open courtyard flanked by two residential buildings. A second temple, which houses a three-dimensional mandala, and a row of eight stupas are located north of the main temple. Other buildings for the monastic middle school and college are located in the surrounding area.

The monastery has developed a master plan to more than double its facilities in order to accommodate more monks studying arts and rituals in the middle school and advanced religious studies in the college.[16]

With its open courtyard and scattered buildings, Nyimalung Goemba feels more like a campus than a monastery.

5

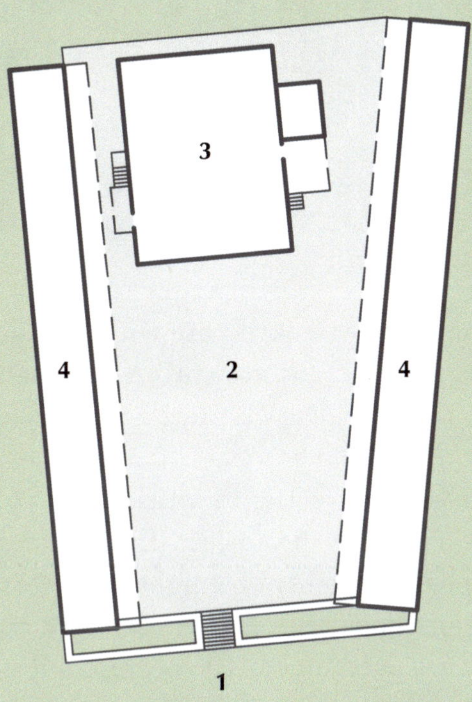

1 Entry
2 Courtyard
3 Lhakhang below
Goenkhang above
4 Housing
5 Kaling Zhithro Lhakhang

100FT/30.5M

The main temple building is a simple structure with skillfully painted woodwork. The front facade has a wood framework set into the stone wall on the first floor and extends the width of the building on the second floor. The framework is filled with an alternating pattern of plaster panels and wood windows.

The framework is decorated with jewels in lotuses and chains of thunder bolts which are known as *dorjes* in Bhutanese and *vajras* in Sanskrit. The jewel represents spiritual wealth and the thunder bolt represents the indestructibility of enlightenment. The thunder bolt is one of the most important symbols of Vajrayana Buddhism and is used in a number of rituals. In some rituals the thunder bolt and the bell are used together to represent the male quality of method and the female quality of wisdom.

The top row of plaster panels on each floor is decorated with strands of jewels and the bottom row of wood panels on each floor is decorated with the *eight auspicious symbols* (pp. 88–89), the offerings ancient Indian gods made to the Buddha when he achieved enlightenment.

Thunder
bolt
Jewels
Jewel in
lotus

DZONGS

Punakha Dzong

Simtokha Dzong

According to legend, the Zhabdrung subdued and banished into a rock a demon that had been harming people traveling between the Thimphu and Punakha valleys. To ensure that the demon could not escape, he built Simtokha Dzong (dzong on top of the demon's stomach).

Completed in 1631, Simtokha Dzong was the first dzong built by the Zhabdrung while unifying Bhutan. With its large three-story mandala-shaped tower and small courtyard enclosed within a two-story building, it is more like a fortified monastery than a fortified district seat. While later dzongs are more commanding, Simtokha Dzong is an impressive statement of the Zhabdrung's intent to take control of the region.

Simtokha Dzong is located on a hill at the southern end of the Thimphu Valley, where the roads to Thimphu and Punakha meet in western Bhutan. It was temporarily captured and partially burned during an attack a few years after it was built, and has been restored and modified a number of times since. Today it houses a monastic college.

For comparison to both other monasteries and dzongs, the plan on the right is shown in two scales—the larger version matches monastery plans in the previous section, and the smaller version matches dzong plans in this section.

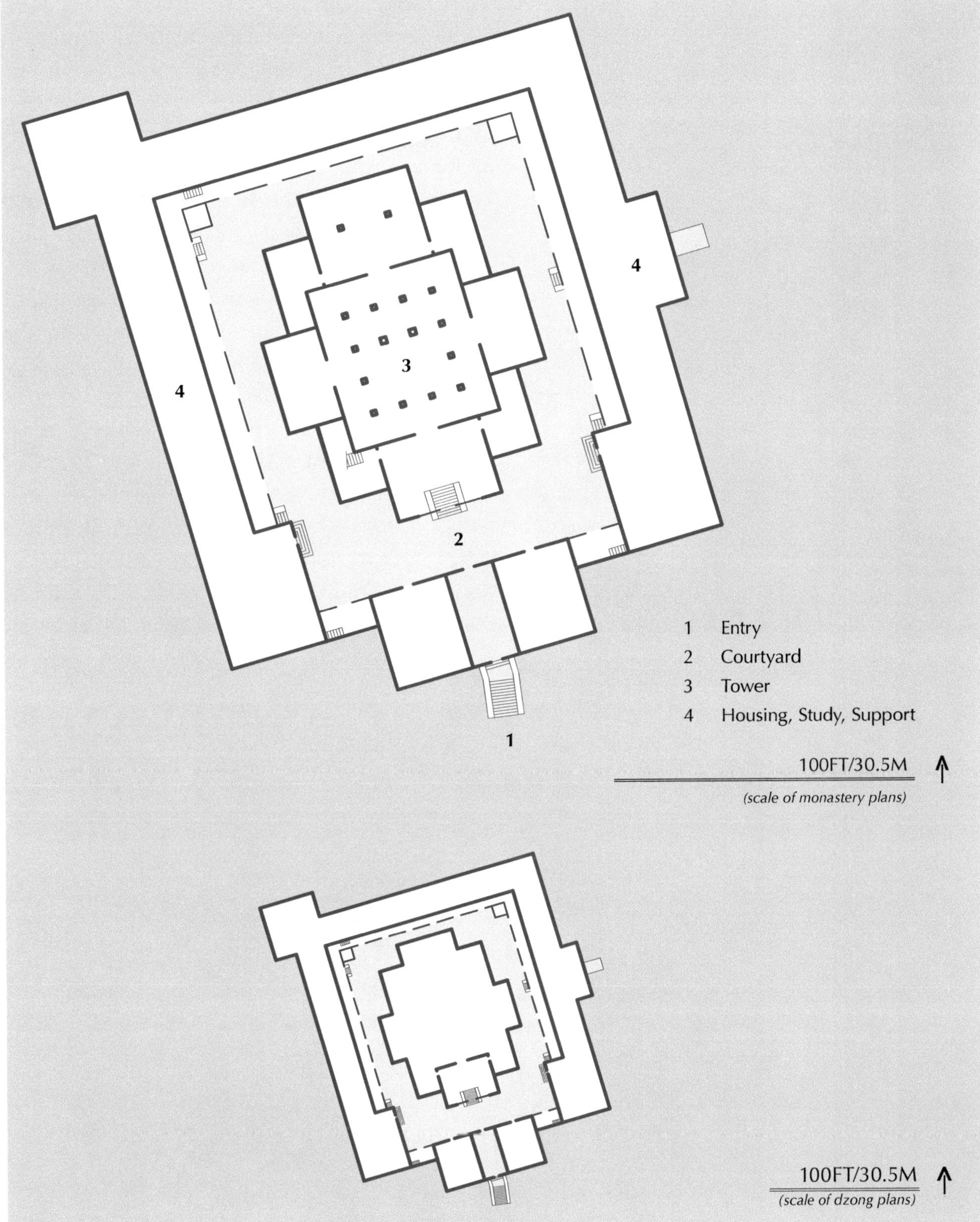
4
4
3
2
1
1 Entry
2 Courtyard
3 Tower
4 Housing, Study, Support
100FT/30.5M
(scale of monastery plans)
100FT/30.5M
(scale of dzong plans)

Although configured like a monastery, Simtokha Dzong has defensive features similar to later dzongs, including exterior walls with few openings, and a raised entry and courtyard originally reached by a ladder that could be pulled up for security.

As shown on the left, a two-story arcade that fronts living spaces lining the exterior wall wraps tightly around the central tower. The arcade is raised a few feet above the courtyard so the basement windows can open onto the courtyard rather than to the exterior, where they would be more vulnerable to attack.

As shown below, the central tower and assembly halls front a small courtyard. Each assembly hall has an entry door (*mago*) decorated with a *dharma wheel*, symbolizing the Buddha's teaching. Since footwear is not worn inside, the front steps are frequently covered with sandals that have been kicked off by monks as they enter.

Punakha Dzong

While camping at the confluence of the Pho and Mo rivers, the Zhabdrung had a dream in which Guru Rinpoche (Padmasambhava) prophesied he would build a dzong below a hill shaped like an elephant. Realizing the mountain north of his camp site looked like an elephant, the Zhabdrung built this dzong on the site. Punakha Dzong is officially known as Punthang Dechen Phodrang (palace of great happiness).

Completed in 1637, Punakha Dzong is the second and largest dzong the Zhabdrung built. It was designed to house the Ranjung Karsapani, the sacred relic he brought from Tibet, and a large monastic community. The dzong has been damaged by fire, flood, and earthquake, and has been renovated and expanded within its outer walls a number of times. It was Bhutan's winter capital until the 1950s and remains the district seat and the winter home of the state monk body.

The dzong is prominently located at the confluence of the Pho (father) and Mo (mother) rivers in the Punakha Valley in western Bhutan. The north courtyard houses the district government offices. The tower separates the north and middle courtyards, and houses several temples, including the Tse Lhakhang, where the Ranjung Karsapani is kept. The middle courtyard houses monks' quarters and the south courtyard houses the monks' assembly halls and temples.

The dzong is both formidable and grand. It's sheer size and defensive might are impressive and design and artisanship are stunning.

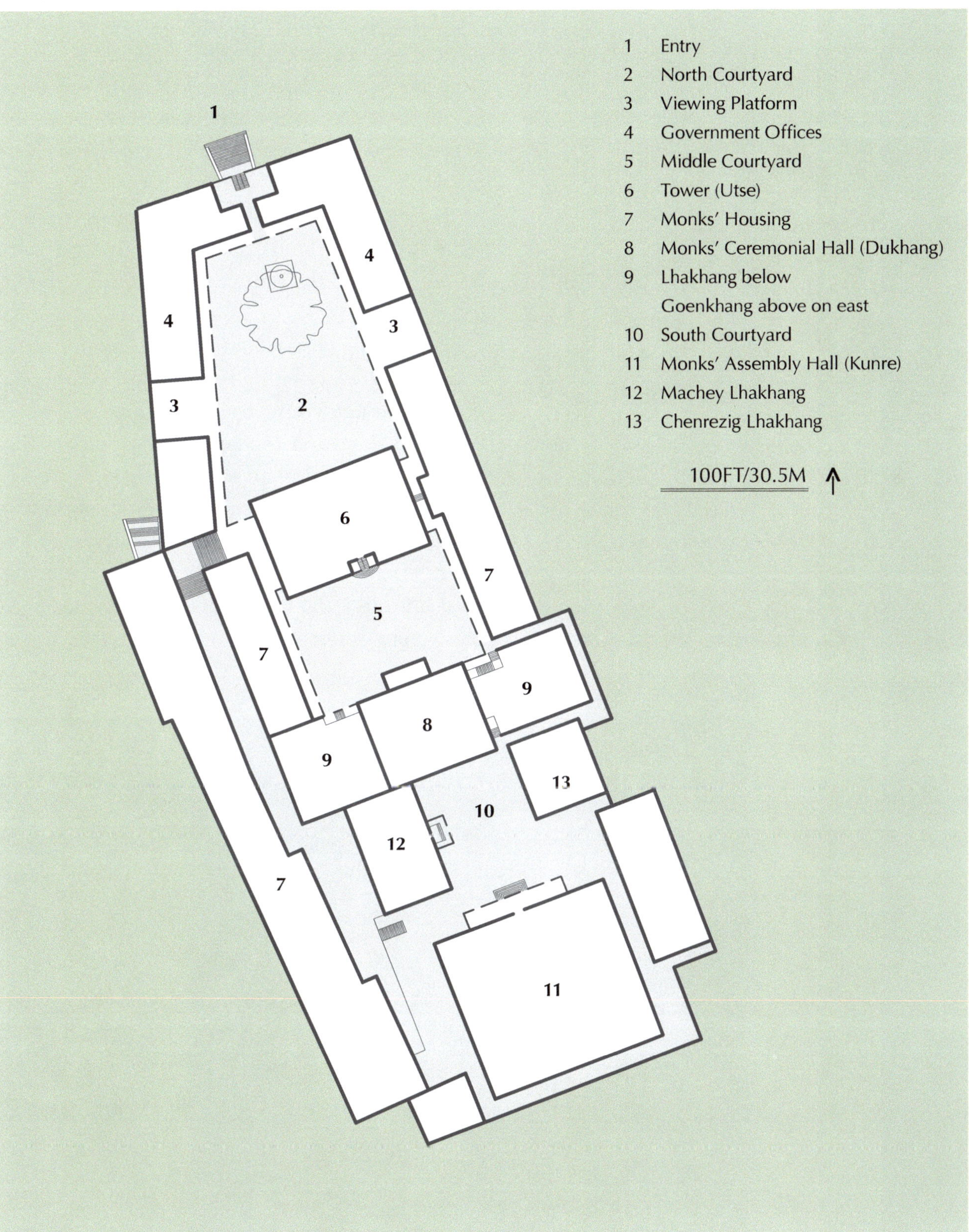
1
2
3
4
4
3
3
6
7
5
7
9
9
8
13
10
12
7
11
1 Entry
2 North Courtyard
3 Viewing Platform
4 Government Offices
5 Middle Courtyard
6 Tower (Utse)
7 Monks' Housing
8 Monks' Ceremonial Hall (Dukhang)
9 Lhakhang below
Goenkhang above on east
10 South Courtyard
11 Monks' Assembly Hall (Kunre)
12 Machey Lhakhang
13 Chenrezig Lhakhang
100FT/30.5M

Punakha Dzong is an impressive defensive structure. Located on a narrow spit between the two rivers, the dzong was originally protected by an outer wall and a watchtower on the north, and cantilever bridges and walls along the rivers on the east and west. Although the outer fortifications no longer exist and the spit is twice as wide (due to a flood that altered the course of the Pho River), the dzong still has a commanding presence.

The dzong has tall and massive tapered stone walls, with few openings on the first and second floors. The entry and courtyard are located on the third floor and are reached by ladders that could be removed in an attack.

The tower (*utse*) is a rectangular structure that rises five stories above the courtyard. The main temple is located a story above the courtyard and, like the dzong entry, is reached by a removable ladder.

Punakha Dzong is also an impressive religious and civic building that is still shared by monks and government officials, who each wear traditional dress—red robes for the monks, and ghos (men) and kiras (women) with ceremonial sashes for the officials.

The sizable north and middle courtyards are enclosed by two-story wood arcades fronting government offices and monk quarters that line the inside of the dzong's exterior walls.

The woodwork is beautifully carved and painted. The first-floor arcade has a traditional cornice with rows of staggered joist ends and columns with scroll-shaped top brackets. The second-floor arcade has large posts that support a raised roof and deep overhangs, and a traditional wood railing with jewel-shaped newel posts and hourglass-shaped panels. The columns on both floors are decorated with colorful round jewels that symbolize spiritual wealth.

The monks' assembly hall (kunre) shown above and Chenrezig Lhakhang shown below are elegant stone structures with bold and richly decorated woodwork.

Om mani padme hum hrih is featured prominently on the header and frame of Chenrezig Lhakhang's balcony windows. The mantra om mani padme hum is attributed to Chenrezig (Avalokiteshvara in Sanskrit), the bodhisattva of compassion; it refers to ultimate truth and the means to realize it. Described in more detail on page 94, the mantra is written in an ancient Indian ceremonial script, and the addition of the syllable hrih, is understood to complete and activate it.

Paro Dzong

In the fifteenth century a descendant of the founder of the Drukpa school in Bhutan constructed a building above the Paro River. In 1645 his descendants gave the building to the Zhabdrung, who replaced it with Paro Dzong. It is officially called the Rinchen Pung Dzong (dzong on a heap of jewels). It was rebuilt after a fire in 1915 and today houses the district government offices and a monastic community.

The dzong is prominently located on a bluff overlooking the Paro Valley in western Bhutan. It has good visibility of the valley and easy access to the river below for water, but due to the terrain would have been difficult to attack. For additional protection, it had a watchtower (*ta dzong*) on the hill above it, an outer wall, a walled path to the river, and a removable cantilever bridge crossing the river. The watchtower is now a museum.

The dzong has two courtyards that step down the hill and are separated by a tower. The upper courtyard houses the district government offices and the senior monk quarters, and the lower courtyard houses the novice monk quarters and other monastic facilities. The tower houses a series of temples.

With its location overlooking the valley and its simple but elegant configuration—a central tower surrounded by a rectangular building, and beautiful courtyards that step down the hill—Paro Dzong has a majestic presence.

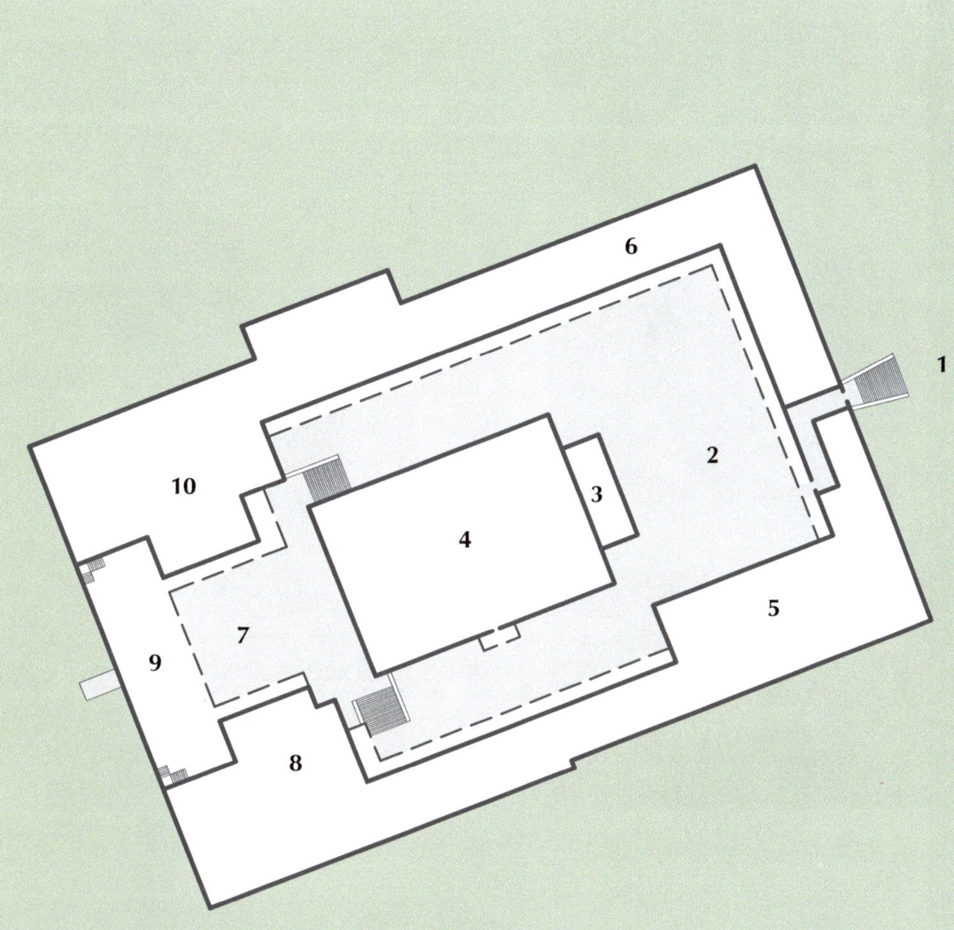

1 Entry
2 Upper Courtyard
3 Chuchizhey Lhakhang
4 Tower (Utse)
5 Government Offices
6 Monks' Housing
7 Lower Courtyard
8 Monks' Assembly Hall (Kunre) below
Monks' Housing above
9 Porch overlooking valley
10 Monks' Prayer Hall (Dukhang) below
Monks' Housing above

100FT/30.5M 

The upper courtyard has a two-story wood arcade with traditional cornices, columns, and railings richly decorated with motifs and notations, many of which are Buddhist symbols. The cornice header is decorated with moons that symbolize method. The upper row of joist ends feature the letter *hum,* which symbolizes the unity of method and wisdom, alternating with the *lotus,* which symbolizes purity or enlightenment. The lower row contains the letter *hrih,* which refers to the mantra om mani padme hum, alternating with the lotus in a rosette form. The column is decorated with a *triple jewel*—which symbolizes the Buddha, his teaching, and the monastic community—in a lotus.

Chuchizhey Lhakhang at the base of the tower, is decorated with the *eight auspicious symbols,* the offerings made by ancient Indian gods to the Buddha when he achieved enlightenment. Each is shown and described on pages 88 and 89.

Trongsa Dzong

In 1543 Ngagi Wangchuk, a Tibetan Drukpa monk, built a temple on a spur high above the Mangde River. His disciples built a small community around the temple, and the community became known as Trong-sar (new village). In 1647, Ngagi Wangchuk's great-grandson, the Zhabdrung, built a dzong on the site. The dzong was the seat of the Trongsa Penlop, one of Bhutan's three powerful regional governors. Minjur Tenpa, the first Trongsa Penlop, led the effort to secure control of the central and eastern regions in order to complete Bhutan's unification. By the end of the nineteenth century, Bhutan's penlops had more power than the central government, and in 1907 Ugyen Wangchuk, then the Trongsa Penlop, became the country's first king.

Trongsa Dzong is strategically located on the spur in central Bhutan, and is visible for miles. Bhutan's historic east-west trade route runs through it, which allowed the Trongsa Penlop to control travel and collect taxes. The dzong was expanded a number of times in the eighteenth century, and is now a series of linked buildings and courtyards of varying sizes and shapes that conform to the topography of the spur. Today the dzong houses the district government offices and a monastic community, and its watchtower houses a museum.

The complex has the powerful presence of a fortress from the exterior, yet inside it feels like a hilltop village.

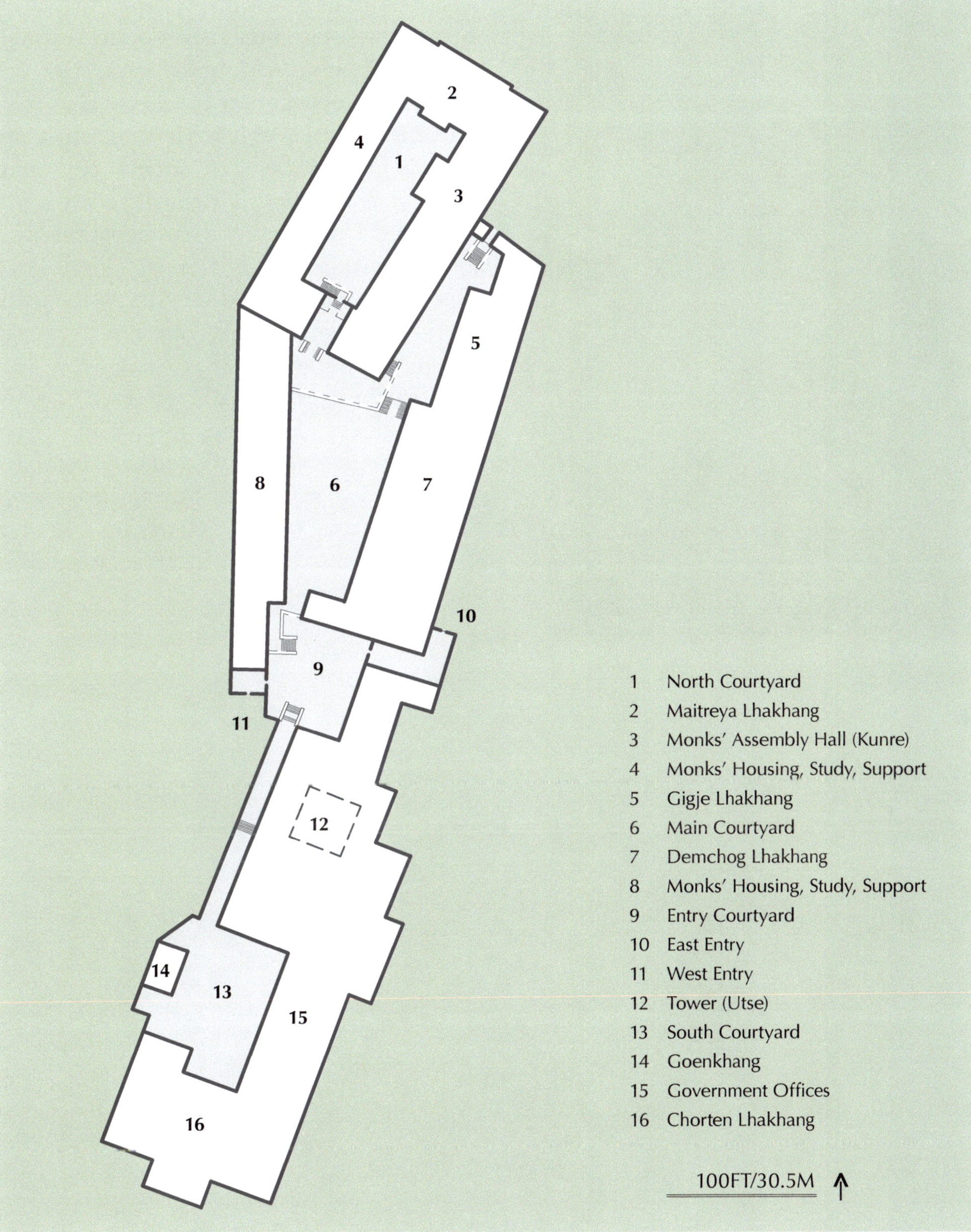
2
4
1
3
5
8
6
7
10
9
11
12
14
13
15
16
1 North Courtyard
2 Maitreya Lhakhang
3 Monks' Assembly Hall (Kunre)
4 Monks' Housing, Study, Support
5 Gigje Lhakhang
6 Main Courtyard
7 Demchog Lhakhang
8 Monks' Housing, Study, Support
9 Entry Courtyard
10 East Entry
11 West Entry
12 Tower (Utse)
13 South Courtyard
14 Goenkhang
15 Government Offices
16 Chorten Lhakhang
100FT/30.5M

The old trail climbs steeply from the valley below to the west entry shown on the left and into the entry courtyard shown on the right.

Although dzongs now have some electricity and running water, and modern materials are available in local shops, the monks' daily routines and preparations for rituals follow traditional practices. One of the traditional practices is wood block printing; the monks print large prayer flags and hang them to dry in the entry courtyard. These prayer flags are used at dzongs and other institutions.

While the dzong initially appears to be a homogeneous complex, closer inspection reveals an eclectic mix of courtyards and buildings built and expanded over time. The tower, smaller than most dzong towers, is likely to have been a sixteenth-century temple that was increased in height as the dzong grew.

Jakar Dzong

In 1549, after founding a temple in Trongsa, Ngagi Wangchuk, a Tibetan Drukpa monk, came to the Chokhor Valley to build a monastery. It is said that, as construction began, a white bird flew from the construction site to a spur. Considering this a good omen, Ngagi Wangchuk built the monastery on the spur instead of on the original site.

In 1646, the Zhabdrung, Ngagi Wangchuk's great-grandson converted the monastery into a dzong. It sustained damage during several Tibetan attacks but survived and was renamed the Jakar Yugyel Dzong (victorious dzong of the white bird). It was damaged again by an earthquake in the nineteenth century, and it is said that is was rebuilt in a smaller form than that of the original. Today Jakar Dzong houses the district government offices and a monastic community.

Jakar Dzong is located on a rise overlooking the Chokhor Valley in central Bhutan. The dzong is a long, narrow structure with a passageway through the tower that connects the east and west courtyards. The watchtower located just west of the dzong is now connected to the dzong with an outer courtyard that houses several small buildings.

While Jakar Dzong exterior appears fairly typical, the interior with its long narrow spaces looks more like an alley than a courtyard building.

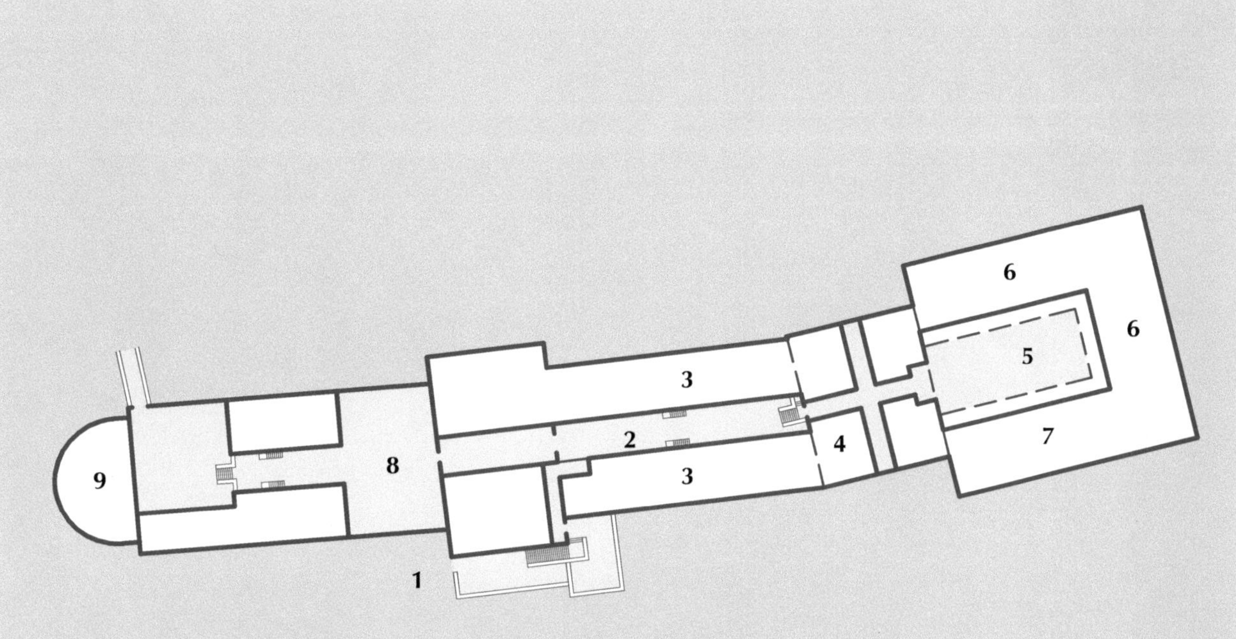

1 Entry
2 West Courtyard
3 Government Offices
4 Tower (Utse)
5 East Courtyard
6 Monks' Housing
7 Monks' Assembly Hall (Kunre)
8 Outer Courtyard and Offices
9 Watchtower, now Offices

100FT/30.5M 

The west courtyard, shown on the left, is unusual in that it was formed by two closely spaced wings that were built like houses with stone walls on the first floor and wood-framed walls on the upper floors, rather than typical dzong wings with two-story wood arcades.

The dzong's woodwork is simple and, with the exception of paint, appears as it did at the beginning of the nineteenth century. The columns (*kachens*) have traditional tapered posts and elongated top brackets (*zhus*). The tops of the columns have a reveal of rosary beads with a garland motif below and a lotus motif above. Some top brackets, like those on the first floor in the image on the left, are in the shape of a simple curve with minimal decoration, while others have a scroll shape with more decoration. The scroll has a typical pattern that extends up into each side of the top bracket to frame a jewel(s), and is expanded or compressed to fit each location.

Trashigang Dzong

Trashigang Dzong was the last dzong built (1656) during Bhutan's unification. Today it houses the district government offices and a monastic community.

Trashigang Dzong (auspicious mountain dzong) is strategically located on a spur high above the gorge where the Gamri and Kulong rivers merge to become the Drongmo River. It is said that the first official structure on the site was a fort built by a local ruler in the twelfth century. The site is visible from and has an excellent view of the surrounding mountains and valleys, though its topography, with a narrow saddle on one side and a steep drop on the other three sides, would have made attack difficult.

Trashigang Dzong is about the size of Simtokha Dzong (pp. 56–59), the first dzong the Zhabdrung built while unifying Bhutan, but it was designed differently. Instead of having a mandala-shaped central tower with a small courtyard surrounded by a relatively low, two-story building, Trashigang Dzong has a rectangular tower integrated into a taller, three-story courtyard building. The layout provides a larger courtyard that could accommodate security and civil needs as well as religious needs. The building's taller walls and an outer fortification also made attack more difficult.

From the exterior, Trashigang Dzong appears to be a small yet grand outpost, and the interior has an efficient feel.

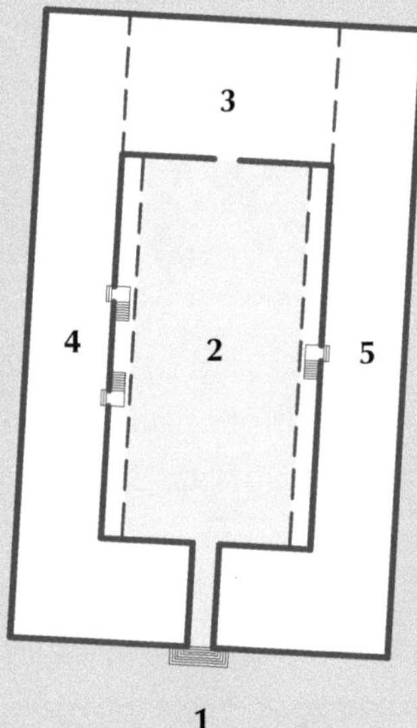

1 Entry below
Monks' Assembly Hall (Kunre) above
2 Courtyard
3 Tower (Utse)
4 Government Offices
5 Monks' Housing

100FT/30.5M

The forecourt, which was originally protected by an outer wall, leads to the entry and into the main courtyard. The four-story tower is located opposite the entry and forms the north side of the courtyard. Three-story buildings form the courtyard's other three sides.

Temples, monasteries, and dzongs typically have a side room or separate temple, known as a *goenkhang*, dedicated to fierce protective deities. Trashigang Dzong's goenkhang is located on the second floor of the tower. Like many goenkhangs, its exterior is decorated with skulls and severed heads, which represent among other things the purification of the mind and of speech.

SYMBOLS

Punakha Dzong

Overview, Wheel, Lotus, and Jewel

Dharma wheel, Jakar Dzong

Dharma wheel, Trongsa Dzong

Lotus, Paro Dzong

Lotus, Paro Dzong

Bhutan's temples, monasteries, and dzongs are decorated with a variety of Buddhist symbols, including motifs, script, animals, figures, and illustrations. Some are common Buddhist symbols, while others are more specific to Mahayana and Vajrayana Buddhist teaching as practiced in Bhutan.

The photographs and descriptions on the following pages are intended to identify a number of these symbols and provide a basic understanding of their significance. Many symbols have layers of meaning that are revealed to and understood by Buddhist practitioners as they advance in their practice. As Dagyab Rinpoche explains in his book *Buddhist Symbols in Tibetan Culture*, Buddhist symbols can be understood at a basic level using definitions, however the right motivation and meditative practice is necessary in order for a practitioner to develop a different level of consciousness and understanding of reality to comprehend the full meaning of symbols.[17]

Perhaps the most common symbols used to decorate Bhutan's temples, monasteries, and dzongs are the wheel, lotus, and jewel.

Dharma means teaching in Sanskrit and thus the **dharma wheel** symbolizes the Buddha's teaching. The circular form represents the completeness of the teaching, and the turning of the wheel represents the transformation of the teaching. The hub symbolizes moral discipline, the spokes symbolize wisdom, and the rim symbolizes concentration. Typically, the wheel has eight spokes, which represent the noble eightfold path to enlightenment. The hub can have three swirls, which represent the Buddha, his teaching, and the monastic community; or four swirls, which represent the four noble truths.

The wheel is one of both the eight auspicious symbols (pp. 88–89) and the seven jewels of royal power (pp. 92–93). It is frequently painted on entry doors as well as incorporated into other decorative woodwork.

Jewel, Paro Dzong

The **lotus** grows from the mud at the bottom of a pond, and blossoms into a beautiful flower on the surface. In Buddhism, the lotus refers to spiritual purity or enlightenment.

One of the eight auspicious symbols (pp. 88–89), it is frequently incorporated into the decoration of cornices and other decorative woodwork. The lotus is shown both in profile and as a rosette, the latter similar to those carved on Indian temples.

Jewel, Trongsa Dzong

The **jewel**, also known as the precious jewel or wish-fulfilling jewel, symbolizes spiritual wealth and wish fulfillment. As described in Bhutan's Department of Tourism's *Icons of Awakened Energy: An Introduction to Bhutanese Iconography*, the jewel represents the capacity to fulfill all material and spiritual aspirations.[18]

The jewel is one of the seven jewels of royal powers (pp. 92–93). It is carved in the form of newel posts, painted on rails and columns, and incorporated into other woodwork.

Triple jewel, Paro Dzong

The **triple jewel** represents the Buddha, his teaching, and the monastic community. As Robert Beer describes in his *Handbook of Tibetan Buddhist Symbols*, it symbolizes the body, speech, and mind of the Buddha—that is, the purified conduct, words, and thoughts of enlightened beings.[19]

The triple jewel is often shown surrounded with a backdrop of flames set in a lotus or on a lotus throne. It is used to decorate column capitals (top of column) and incorporated into other woodwork.

Triple jewel, Punakha Dzong

Eight Auspicious Symbols

The eight auspicious symbols represent the offerings that the ancient Indian gods made to the Buddha when he achieved enlightenment.[20]

These symbols are used in rituals and building decoration. The examples shown decorate Chuchizhey Lhakhang at Paro Dzong (pp. 68–71). Except for the lotus itself, each article is set on a lotus and has a silk ribbon floating around it. The ribbon signifies the Buddha's brilliance and his ability to adapt to any circumstance.

Parasol

The **parasol** became a symbol of status and protection because only royalty and the well-to-do had parasols to protect themselves from the rain and sun. In Buddhism, the parasol represents the Buddha's spiritual power and protection from obstacles, illnesses, and harmful forces.

Two golden fish

The **two golden fish** are a symbol of happiness and fertility. It is said that fish signify happiness because they move freely in water, and fertility because they multiply rapidly. In Buddhism, the two golden fish represent good fortune or salvation from suffering.

Treasure vase

The **treasure vase** is a symbol of wealth. Its form is based on the Indian clay water pot, and its jewel stopper indicates that it is a treasure vase. In Buddhism, the treasure vase symbolizes both spiritual and material prosperity. In the example on the left, the stopper is a triple jewel which represents the Buddha, his teaching, and the monastic community.

Lotus

The **lotus** is a beautiful flower that grows from the mud at the bottom of a pond. In Buddhism, the lotus is a visual metaphor for purity or enlightenment because it is unstained by the mud from which it grows.

Conch shell

The **conch shell** was blown as a horn in battle to demonstrate power and authority. In Buddhism, it represents the renown of the Buddha's teaching.

Endless knot

The **endless knot** is used in many traditions. In Buddhism, it symbolizes the nature of reality, in which everything is interrelated and only exists as part of causes and conditions. The endless knot also symbolizes the Buddha's infinite knowledge.

Dharma wheel & victory banner

The wheel is a symbol of supreme power. In Buddhism, the **dharma wheel** symbolizes the Buddha's teaching. Described in more detail on page 86, the hub symbolizes moral discipline, the spokes wisdom, and the rim concentration.

The **victory banner** (*gyaltshen* in Bhutanese) was originally a military symbol. In Buddhism, it represents the victory of the Buddha's teaching over ignorance, and the wish for permanent happiness.

As shown in the image second from the bottom, the wheel and victory banner are presented in one illustration at Paro Dzong. As shown in the bottom image, the victory banner is used as a roof ornament on temples that have a large number of sacred texts.

Victory banner, Punakha Dzong

Eight Auspicious Substances

Mirror

The eight auspicious substances, also called the eight lucky articles and the eight bringers of good fortune, represent the practices of an enlightened being as delineated in the *noble eightfold path.* These include 1) right insight, 2) right aspiration, 3) right speech, 4) right conduct, 5) right livelihood, 6) right effort, 7) right mindfulness, and 8) right meditation attainment.[21]

The substances are used as offerings in rituals and in building decoration. The examples shown decorate the courtyard arcade at Tango Goemba (pp. 42–45). Each substance is in an offering bowl and has a silk ribbon floating around it. The ribbon signifies the Buddha's brilliance and his ability to adapt to any circumstance.

Mustard seed

The **mirror** which accurately reflects all things, represents the Buddha's complete understanding of everything and is a symbol of right insight.

Conch shell

Mustard seed was used in rituals to expel demons, which represent hindrances or ignorance of the unenlightened conscience. In Buddhism it represents the right aspiration or view.

The Buddha used mustard seed to teach a woman, distraught by the loss of a child, that death and sorrow are part of life. He asked the woman to collect mustard seed, a common herb, from every home that never had a loss. When she returned empty-handed, the Buddha showed her that she was not alone in her sorrow and that death is an inescapable part of life.

Bilva fruit

The **conch shell** was used as a horn and represents the renown of the Buddha's teaching and right speech.

Curd

Bilva fruit or wood apple was a sacred fruit in ancient India. In Buddhism it represents causes and effects, and symbolizes right action or conduct.

Curd or yogurt was a highly valued food. It represents abandoning negative actions and symbolizes right livelihood.

Durva grass

Durva grass is a hardy plant and a symbol of long life. In Buddhism it symbolizes release from the cycle of rebirth through the right effort.

Precious medicine was a soothing and strengthening medicine made from animal gallstones. It represents removing mental poisons that prevent wisdom and symbolizes right mindfulness.

Precious medicine

Vermilion or cinnabar is a red powder that represents control and symbolizes right concentration or meditation attainment.

Vermilion

Seven Jewels of Royal Power

Chakravartin (wheel turner) was the ancient Indian universal monarch. The Buddha is considered to be the supreme Chakravartin. The seven jewels of royal power represent the universal monarch's qualities—and thus the qualities a practitioner needs to overcome all obstacles and be reborn as a chakravartin.[22]

The seven jewels of royal power are given as offerings of good fortune to religious and civil leaders on special occasions. They are also used in building decoration. The examples shown decorate the lintel above the main entry porch at Gangte Goemba (pp. 46–49).

Precious wheel

The **precious wheel** represents the Buddha's teaching, the means by which spiritual power is gained and maintained. As Dagyab Rinpoche states in his book *Buddhist Symbols in Tibetan Culture*, "Just as the king, with the aid of the wheel, has conquered the entire earth, so too the Buddha, through the power of the path, has cut through the bonds of the demons."[23]

Precious jewel

The **precious jewel** is like a crystal ball in that it lets one see and understand all. Thus the precious jewel represents the ability to see and understand all through the means of the Buddha's teaching.

Precious queen

The **precious queen**, like a goddess, is both beautiful and virtuous. She represents the feminine side of the conscience and the joy of enlightenment.

Precious minister

The **precious minister** is invaluable; he can understand and carry out a king's intent without delay or harm to others. Thus in Buddhism, the precious minister represents the ability to implement thoughts without hindrance.

Precious horse

The **precious horse** has a fast and effortless gallop and thus represents unfaltering speed.

Precious general

The **precious general** symbolizes the wrathful power to overcome enemies.

Precious elephant

The **precious elephant** is a powerful yet unflappable and gentle animal. The precious elephant symbolizes the unlimited strength and capabilities of the Buddha.

Script

om ma ni pad me hum

Om mani padme hum (Lantsa script), Punakha Dzong

Mantras are short prayers "that are thought to subtly alter one's mind".[24] Perhaps the best-known mantra is **om mani padme hum**, which is attributed to Chenrezig (Avalokiteshvara in Sanskrit), the bodhisattva of compassion. His Holiness Tenzin Gyatso, the Fourteenth Dalai Lama, who is recognized as a reincarnation of Chenrezig, explained:

> the meaning of the six syllables is great and vast . . . OM, is composed of three pure letters [that] . . . symbolize the practitioner's impure body, speech, and mind; they also symbolize the pure exalted body, speech and mind of a Buddha. . . . MANI, meaning jewel, symbolizes the factor of method—the altruistic intention to become enlightened, compassion, and love. . . . The two syllables, PADME, meaning lotus, symbolize wisdom. . . . Purity must be achieved by an indivisible unity of method and wisdom, symbolized by the final syllable, HUM, which indicates indivisibility. . . . Thus the six syllables, OM MANI PADME HUM, mean that in dependence on the practice, which is [an] indivisible union of method and wisdom, you can transform your impure body, speech and mind into the pure body, speech, and mind of a Buddha.[25]

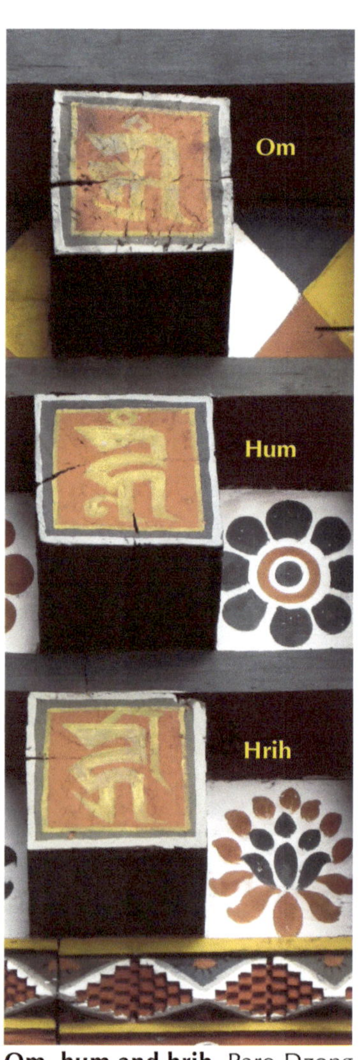

Om, hum and hrih, Paro Dzong

Seed syllables are single-syllable mantras.[26] They are frequently painted—in Lantsa, an ancient ceremonial Indian script—on the projecting joist ends of a cornice over a door or window, or between floors in an arcade. The cornice on the left has a repeating pattern of om, hum, and hrih on the joist ends and a repeating pattern of the diamond pattern of the elements and two forms of the lotus on the background.

All–powerful ten, Punakha Dzong

Om is often the first syllable in a mantra. In some cases it serves as an introduction to what follows and in other cases, such as in the mantra om mani padme hum, it represents the practitioner's impurity and the Buddha's purity.

Hum represents the indivisible unity of method and wisdom. According to Lama Govinda, om represents the potential of attaining Buddhahood, and hum represents Buddhahood made manifest.[27]

All–powerful ten, Peshling Goemba

Hrih is the seed syllable of Opagme (Amitabha in Sanskrit), the Buddha of Infinite Light, and thus represents meditation and compassion. Hrih, which is sometimes added to the end of om mani padme hum to complete and activate the mantra, can also represent the mantra.

Shou, Kyichu Lhakhang

The **all-powerful ten** represent the *Dukhor* (*Kalachakra* in Sanskrit) teaching, which is a Tantric practice used by some Buddhist schools. The all-powerful ten are a composite of stylized letters in Lantsa script. The composite includes the letters ham, ksha, ma, la, wa, ra and ya. The ring of fire represents wisdom. The circle and crescent on top of the composite represent om, the Buddha's purity. The letters e on the left and vam on the right represent the union of method and wisdom required to achieve enlightenment. The letter ham represents enlightened wisdom, and ksha represents deities' body, speech, and mind. The letter ma represents the mandala palace on the top of Mount Meru (center of the universe), and la, wa, ra and ya represent the elements earth, water, fire, and wind around that palace.[28]

The **shou** is derived from the Chinese character for longevity. The vertical form, shown on top in the example on the left, is said to resemble a butterfly and therefore to represent transmutation, resurrection, and immortality. The circular form, shown on the bottom, represents immortality.[29]

Animals, Figures, and Illustrations

The *four power animals* were adapted from ancient Chinese traditions and include the dragon, garuda, snow lion and tiger. They are believed to bring good luck and are often depicted on prayer flags. They are also used as a group or individually in building decoration.

Dragon, Punakha Dzong

The **dragon** (*druk* in Bhutanese) is an ancient Chinese symbol of power and a national symbol of Bhutan. When the Zhabdrung, a Drukpa monk, unified Bhutan, it became known as *Druk Yul* (land of the thunder dragon). According to legend the Drukpa school got its name when Tibetan monk Tsangpa Gyare, looking for a suitable monastery site, heard a dragon thunder. Taking this as a good omen, he built a monastery where he heard the thunder and named the monastery after it.

Garuda, Simtokha Dzong

Garuda is the mythical king of the birds. Within the Nyingmapa school it represents the wrathful form of Guru Rinpoche (Padmasambhava in Sanskrit), the great eighth century CE Buddhist teacher. Carved wood garudas can be found mounted just below the kemar (red band) at the corners of temples or dzong towers.

Snow lion, Paro Dzong

The **snow lion** (*singye* in Bhutanese) represents the joyful and fearless enlightened mind. Carved wood snow lions can be found mounted just below the kemar (red band) at the corners of dzong towers or temples.

The **tiger** is a symbol of fearless strength and confidence.

Tiger, Trashigang Dzong

Kirtimukha, Trongsa Dzong

Kirtimukha (face of glory) is a protective deity in the form of a mythical monster. It is typically shown with one or more jewels spewing from its mouth. The figure of Kirtimukha is used to decorate column capitals and is incorporated in other decorative woodwork.

Mahakala, Tamshing Goemba

Mahakala (Yeshe Goenpo in Bhutanese, great black one) was a protective deity of the Zhabdrung who unified the country and is a primary fierce protective deity of Bhutan.

Typically a fierce protective deity (*chosung* in Bhutanese; *dharmapalas* in Sanskrit) is a pre-Buddhist deity or demon who was subdued and made a protector of Buddhism. As explained in Bhutan's Department of Tourism's *Awakened Energy: An Introduction to Bhutanese Iconography* fierce deities, such as Mahakala, are not symbols of anger or hatred but rather express the "sheer energy and power required to overcome the deep seated and subtle obscurations latent in ourselves." [30]

Mahakala, Punakha Dzong

Heads and **skulls** refer to the letting go of obstacles and are used to decorate the exterior of a goenkhang.

Heads & Skulls, Trongsa Dzong

The **four guardians** are ancient Indian mythological figures who the Buddha made protectors against demons. The guardian of the north (*Namthose*) has yellow skin and holds a victory banner and a mongoose spewing jewels, which represent his role as a protector and a granter of wealth. The guardian of the east (*Yulkhorsung*) has white skin and plays a lute, which symbolizes harmony. The guardian of the south (*Phagchep*) has blue skin and holds a sword, which represents his role as a commander. The guardian of the west (*Chenmizang*) has red skin and holds a snake and a stupa, which symbolize his role as protector of waters and relics. The four guardians are often painted at a temple or dzong entry for protection and are prayed to for riches.[31]

The guardian of the north, Paro Dzong

The guardian of the east, Paro Dzong

The guardian of the west, Paro Dzong

The guardian of the south, Paro Dzong

The story of the **four friends** tells how the elephant, the monkey, the rabbit, and the bird worked together to plant, cultivate, and harvest a fruit tree. The story is derived from a parable the Buddha told his disciples to teach respect and cooperation. The four friends are painted at a dzong or temple entry.

Four Friends, Punakha Dzong

The demon holding the **wheel of life** represents impermanence. At the hub of the wheel are three animals that represent the poisons that cause rebirth: The bird represents greed or attachment, the snake represents anger, and the pig represents ignorance. Around the wheel are the six realms of life into which people can be reborn depending on their past lives. These include the demigod, god, and human realms on the top, and the angry god, hell, animal realms on the bottom. Around the rim are the twelve conditions that lead to the cycle of rebirth.[32]

The wheel of life is used for education and frequently painted at a temple entry.

Wheel of Life, Trongsa Dzong

The **mandala**, which roughly means circle in Sanskrit, originally was simply a sacred space. In Buddhism a mandala is a geometric diagram used to aid a practitioner in detailed visualization. It typically has of a series of nested circles and squares with a deity in a palace at the center of the diagram. The palace has a square plan with a projecting entry gate on each side. The shape is derived from a square set on a crossed thunder bolt (crossed *dorje* or crossed *vajra*) and symbolizes the stability, or unshakable foundation of the Buddha's teaching.

In addition to being used as an aid in meditation, the mandala is painted on the ceiling over an entry, as it was in early Indian temples, to bless those who walk under it.

Mandala, Buli Lhakhang

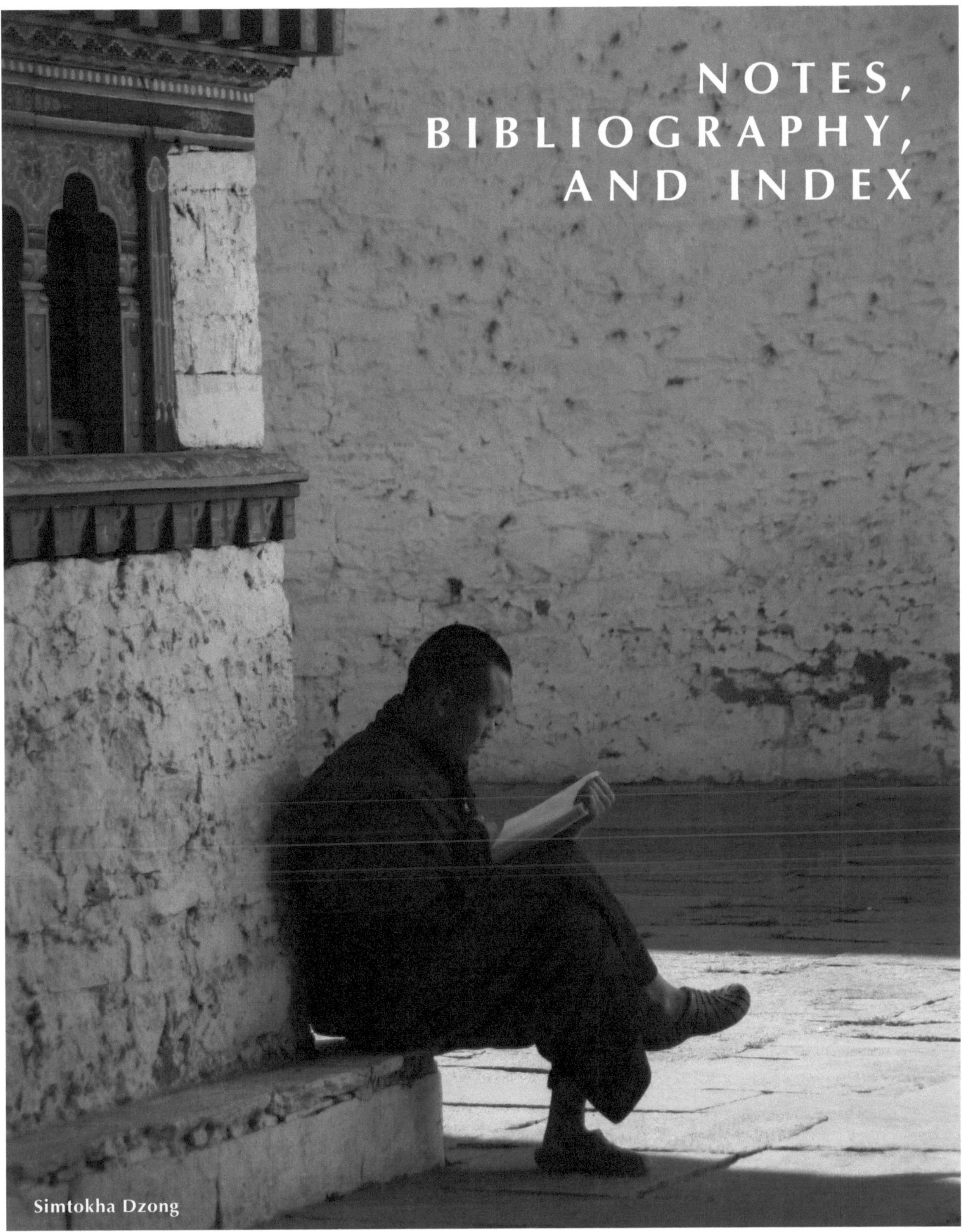

NOTES, BIBLIOGRAPHY, AND INDEX

Simtokha Dzong

Notes

1 See *Columbia Chronologies of Asian History and Culture*, ed. John Stewart Bowman, for a regional overview; and Sam Van Schaik, *Tibet: A History*, and David L. Snellgrove and Hugh Edward Richardson, *A Cultural History of Tibet*, for a detailed understanding of Tibet's history.

2 See Michael Aris, *Bhutan: The Early History of the Himalayan Kingdom*, and Françoise Pommaret, "The Birth of a Nation," in *Bhutan: Mountain Fortress of the Gods*, for a detailed understanding of Bhutan's history.

3 Aris, *Bhutan*, 215.

4 See John Power, *Introduction to Tibetan Buddhism* (rev. ed.), and Christian Schicklgruber, *The Tower of Trongsa: Religion and Power in Bhutan*, for a detailed understanding of Buddhism in India, Tibet, and Bhutan.

5 Power, *Introduction*, 63–71, and Schicklgruber, *The Tower of Trongsa*, 116.

6 Power, *Introduction*, 105–106, 249–50.

7 Andre Alexander, *The Temples of Lhasa: Tibetan Buddhist Architecture from the 7th to the 21st Centuries*, vol. 1, 277.

8 Françoise Pommaret, *Bhutan—Himalayan Mountain Kingdom*, 91.

9 See Peter Harrison, *Fortress Monasteries of the Himalayas: Tibet, Ladakh, Nepal and Bhutan*, and Ingun Bruskeland Amundsen, "On Bhutanese and Tibetan Dzongs," in *Journal of Bhutan Studies* 5, for additional information.

10 Dorji Yangki, "Sacred Architectural Heritage in Bhutan: Traditional Approaches and Emerging Concepts for Conservation," in *The Dragon's Gift: The Sacred Arts of Bhutan*, ed. Bartholomew and Johnson, 115.

11 Department of Urban Housing and Development [Royal Government of Bhutan]. *Traditional Architecture Guide*, 7–9.

12 Pommaret, Bhutan, 82.

13 "About Prayer Wheels," in *Tibetan Prayer Wheels*.

14 H. E. Gangteng Tulku Rinpoche, "The Jewel Rosary of the Successive Incarnations of Gangteng Tulku: The Lineage Holders of Gangteng Sangngak Chöling Monastery."

15 Stephen Adell, "Thubten Shaydrup Darjay Choling, Nyimalung Monastery."

16 Gandhara Designs, "Proposed expansion and redevelopment of the existing Dratshang at Nimalung in Bumthang, Kingdom of Bhutan."

17 Loden Sherap Dagyab Rinpoche, *Buddhist Symbols in Tibetan Culture: An Investigation of the Nine Best-Known Groups of Symbols*, xv–xvii, 3–13.

18 Department of Tourism, Royal Government of Bhutan. *Icons of Awakened Energy, An Introduction to Bhutanese Iconography*, by Kunsang D. Dorji, 50.

19 Robert Beer, *The Handbook of Tibetan Symbols*, 49.

20 See Dagyab Rinpoche, *Buddhist Symbols*, 16–38; Robert Beer, *The Encyclopedia of Tibetan Symbols* and Motifs, 171–85; and Meher McArthur, *Reading Buddhist Art: An Illustrated Guide to Buddhist Signs and Symbols*, 119, for detailed descriptions of the eight auspicious symbols.

21 See Dagyab Rinpoche, *Buddhist Symbols*, 40–63, and Beer, *Encyclopedia*, 187–90, for detailed descriptions of the eight auspicious substances. See Power, *Introduction*, 63–71, and Schicklgruber, *The Tower of Trongsa*, 116 for detailed description of the eight fold noble path.

22 See Dagyab Rinpoche, *Buddhist Symbols*, 64–88, and Beer, *Encyclopedia*, 160–63, for detailed descriptions of the seven jewels of royal power.

23 Dagyab Rinpoche, *Buddhist Symbols*, 68.

24 Power, Introduction, 22

25 His Holiness Tenzin Gyatso, the Fourteenth Dalai Lama of Tibet, "On the meaning of OM MANI PADME HUM. The jewel is in the lotus or praise to the jewel in the lotus."

26 "Bija-seed syllables," in *Visible Mantra*.

27 "The Seed Syllable Om," in *Visible Mantra*.

28 "The Tenfold Powerful One."

29 Beer, *Encyclopedia*, 358.

30 Department of Tourism. *Icons*, 112, 117.

31 Schicklgruber, *The Tower of Trongsa*, 39–41.

32 Schicklgruber, *The Tower of Trongsa*, 115.

Bibliography

Adell, Stephen. "Thubten Shaydrup Darjay Choling, Nyimalung Monastery." Accessed August 2014 at www.nyimalungmonastery.org/NL%20publication-web%20compact-links.pdf.

Alexander, Andre. *The Temples of Lhasa: Tibetan Buddhist Architecture from the 7th to the 21st Centuries.* Vol. 1 of Tibet's Heritage Foundation Conservation Inventory. Chicago: Serindia Publications, 2005.

Amundsen, Ingun Bruskeland. "On Bhutanese and Tibetan Dzongs," *Journal of Bhutan Studies* 5 (Winter 2001). Accessed 2014 at www.bhutanstudies.org.

Ardussi, John. "Formation of the State of Bhutan ('Brug gzhung) in the 17th Century and Its Tibetan Antecedents," *Journal of Bhutan Studies* 11 (Winter 2004). Accessed 2014 at www.bhutanstudies.org.

____. "Observations on the Political Organisation of Western Bhutan in the 14th Century, as Revealed in Records of the 'Ba' Ra Ba Sect." In *Impressions of Bhutan and Tibetan Art: Tibetan Studies III* (PIATS 2000: Tibetan Studies), 5–22. Boston: Köln, Brill, 2002.

Aris, Michael. *Bhutan: The Early History of the Himalayan Kingdom.* Warminster, England: Aris & Phillips, 1979.

____. *The Raven Crown: The Origins of Buddhist Monarchy in Bhutan.* London: Serindia Publications, 1998.

____. *Views of Medieval Bhutan: The Diary and Drawings of Samuel Davis, 1783.* Washington D.C.: Smithsonian Institution Press, and London: Serindia Publications, 1982.

Bartholomew, Terese Tse, and John Johnston. *The Dragon's Gift: The Sacred Arts of Bhutan.* Chicago: Serindia Publications, 2008.

Beer, Robert. *The Encyclopedia of Tibetan Symbols and Motifs.* Boston: Shambala Publications, 1999.

____. *The Handbook of Tibetan Symbols.* Boston: Shambala, 2003.

Bowman, John Stewart, ed. *Columbia Chronologies of Asian History and Culture.* New York: Columbia UP, 2000.

Bhutan, Bulletin of the Asian Cultural Centre for UNESCO, no. 35 (1983).

Bhutan Cultural Atlas. "Articles and Sites and Structures" and associated pages. Accessed August 2014 at www.bhutanculturalatlas.org/topics/culture/sites-structures.

Crowther, Geoff, Hugh Finaly, Prakash A Raj, and Tony Wheeler. *India: A Travel Survival Kit.* 4th ed. Victoria, Australia: Lonely Planet Publications, 1990.

Dagyab Rinpoche, Loden Sherap. *Buddhist Symbols in Tibetan Culture: An Investigation of the Nine Best-Known Groups of Symbols.* Boston: Wisdom Publications, 1995.

Department of Tourism, Royal Government of Bhutan. *Icons of Awakened Energy: An Introduction to Bhutanese Iconography,* consultant (author) Kunsang D. Dorji. 2003.

Department of Urban Housing and Development, [Royal Government of Bhutan]. *Traditional Architecture Guide.* Accessed 2014 at www.mowhs.gov.bt/wp-content/uploads/2010/11/TRADITIONAL-ARCHITECTURE1.pdf.

Department of Works, Housing and Roads, Royal Government of Bhutan. *An Introduction to Traditional Architecture of Bhutan,* author Dawa Tsering. 1993.

Di Mattia, Marialaura. "Indo-Tibetan Schools of Art and Architecture in the Western Himalayas: The Instance of Riba in Kinnaur." In *Impressions of Bhutan and Tibetan Art: Tibetan Studies III* (PIATS 2000: Tibetan Studies 2), 91–112. Boston: Köln, Brill, 2002.

Dorji, Kinley, and Rinzin Wangchuk. "Gangteng Goenpa—The Gem of Phobjikha," Kuensel Online, October 8, 2008. Accessed 2014 at www.buddhistchannel.tv/index.php?id=40,7223,0,0,1,0#.U-vp9SifMqZ.

Dujardin, Marc. "From Fortress to Farmhouse: A Living Architecture." In *Bhutan: Mountain Fortress of the Gods,* 61–99. Boston: Shambhala Publications, 1997.

____. "From Living to Propelling Monument: the Monastery-Fortress (dzong) as Vehicle of Cultural Transfer in Contemporary Bhutan." In *Journal of Bhutan Studies* 2:2 (Winter 2000). Accessed 2014 at www.bhutanstudies.org.

Gandhara Designs. "Proposed expansion and redevelopment of the existing Dratshang at Nimalung in Bumthang, Kingdom of Bhutan." Accessed on the web.

Gelay, Karma. Maintenance Plan for Religious Buildings in Bhutan Using Buli Lhakhang Case Study for the Advanced Training Programme Conservation and Management of Historic Buildings, Conducted by the Department of Architectural Restoration and Conservation, Department of Housing Development and Management. Sweden: Lund University and SIDA. Accessed 2014 at www.lth.se/filead min/hdm/alumni/papers/cmhb2005/cmhb2005-18.pdf.

Google. Google earth views of Bhutan. Accessed 2014 at www.google.com/earth.

Gyalwang Drukpa. Tsangpa Gyare Yeshe Dorje. Accessed 2014 at www.drukpa.org/index.php/en/my-gurus/60-drukpa-lineage/the-past-reincarnations/286-tsangpa-gyare-yeshe-dorje.

H. E. Gangteng Tulku Rinpoche, "The Jewel Rosary of the Successive Incarnations Gangteng Tulku: The Lineage Holders of Gangteng Sangngak Chöling Monastery," January 2009. Accessed 2014 at www.yeshekho.ca/Jewel_Rosary.pdf.

Harle, J. C. *The Art and Architecture of the Indian Subcontinent*. Harmondsworth, Middlesex, England: Penguin, 1986.

Harrison, Peter. *Fortress Monasteries of the Himalayas, Tibet, Ladakh, Nepal and Bhutan*. Vol. 104 of the Fortress Series edited by Marcus Cowper, Kindle e-book.

Himalayan Art. "Buddhist Protector: Four Guardian Kings Page." Accessed 2014 at http://www.himalayanart.org/search/set.cfm?setID=159.

His Holiness Tenzin Gyatso, the Fourteenth Dalai Lama of Tibet. "On the meaning of OM MANI PADME HUM: The jewel is in the lotus or praise to the jewel in the lotus." Accessed 2014 at www.sacred-texts.com/bud/tib/omph.htm.

International Kalachakra Network. "The Tenfold Powerful One." Accessed 2014 at www.kalachakranet.org/kalachakra_tantra_10-fold_powerful.html.

Kuenleg, Tshenyid Lopen. "A Brief History of Tango Monastery," in *Journal of Bhutan Studies* 2:1 (Summer 2000). Accessed 2014 at www.bhutanstudies.org.

Laird, Thomas. *The Story of Tibet: Conversations with the Dalai Lama*. New York: Grove Press, 2006.

Little Bhutan. "Dzongs and Fortresses of Bhutan" and associated pages. Accessed 2014 at www.bhutandzongs.com.

Mayhew, Bradley, Joseph Bindloss, and Stan Armington. *Nepal*. Oakland: Lonely Planet, 2006.

Mayhew, Bradley, Lindsay Brown, and Anirban Mahapatra. *Bhutan*, 4th ed. Oakland: Lonely Planet, 2011.

Mayhew, Bradley, Michael Kohn, Daniel McCrohan, and John V. Bellezza. *Tibet*, 8th ed. Oakland: Lonely Planet, 2011.

McArthur, Meher. *Reading Buddhist Art: An Illustrated Guide to Buddhist Signs and Symbols*. New York: Thames and Hudson, 2002.

Olschak, Blanche C. *Ancient Bhutan: A Study on Early Buddhism in the Himalayas*. Zurich: Swiss Foundation for Alpine Research, 1979.

Olschak, Blanche C., Augusto Gansser, and Emil M. Buhrer. *Himalayas*. Lucerne: Motovun, 1987.

Omiglot, the online encyclopedia of writing systems & languages. "Ranjana script." Accessed 2014 at www.omniglot.com/writing/ranjana.htm.

Pommaret, Françoise. *Bhutan: A Kingdom of the Eastern Himalayas*. Boston: Shambhala Publications, 1985.

____. *Bhutan—Himalayan Mountain Kingdom*. Hong Kong: Odyssey Books & Guides, 2009.

____. "The Birth of a Nation." In *Bhutan: Mountain Fortress of the Gods*, 179–207. Boston: Shambhala Publications, 1997.

____. "Ethnic Mosaic: Peoples of Bhutan." In *Bhutan: Mountain Fortress of the Gods*, 43–59. Boston: Shambhala Publications, 1997.

Power, John. *Introduction to Tibetan Buddhism*, revised ed. Ithaca, 2007.

Rawson, Philip S. *Sacred Tibet*. New York: Thames and Hudson, 1991.

Schaik, Sam Van. *Tibet: A History*. New Haven: Yale University Press, 2011.

Schicklgruber, Christian. *The Tower of Trongsa: Religion and Power in Bhutan*. Ghent: Snoeck Publishers, 2009.

Smillie, Robin. "Tsa-Tsa, miniature stupas of Bhutan" in Tashi Delek, July–September 2009. Accessed 2014 at www.rainbowphototours.com/pdf/2009/Tashi_july09.pdf.

Snellgrove, David L., and Hugh Edward Richardson. *A Cultural History of Tibet*. Boston: Shambhala Publications, 1995.

Tibetan Heritage Fund. "Research" and associated pages. Accessed 2014 at www.tibetheritagefund.org/pages/research.php.

Tibetan Prayer Wheels. "About Prayer Wheels." Accessed 2014 at www.tibetanprayerwheels.com/about-prayer-wheels.html.

"Trongsa Dzong Plan." Accessed 2014 at www.p-b-export.at/db_consultants/upload.../403__testimonial.pdf.

Visible Mantra. "Bija-seed syllables" and associated pages. Accessed 2014 at www.visiblemantra.org.

Wikipedia. "Architecture of Bhutan" and individual Bhutanese and Tibetan temple, monastery, and dzong pages. Accessed 2014 at www.wikipedia.org.

Yangki ,Dorji. "Sacred Architectural Heritage in Bhutan: Traditional Approaches and Emerging Concepts for Conservation." In *The Dragon's Gift: The Sacred Arts of Bhutan*, edited by Terese Tse Bartholomew and John Johnson, 114–125. Chicago: Serindia Publications, 2008.

Index

www.ingramcontent.com/pod-product-compliance
Lightning Source LLC
LaVergne TN
LVHW070216110826
845147LV00003B/582
* 9 7 8 0 9 9 6 6 6 3 9 0 8 *